The Life
of the
World to Come

The Albert Cardinal Meyer Lectures

The Life
of the
World to Come

NEAR-DEATH EXPERIENCE
AND CHRISTIAN HOPE

Carol Zaleski

New York *Oxford* OXFORD UNIVERSITY PRESS 1996

Oxford University Press

Oxford   New York
Athens   Auckland   Bangkok
Calcutta   Cape Town   Dar es Salaam   Delhi
Florence   Hong Kong   Istanbul   Karachi
Kuala Lumpur   Madras   Madrid   Melbourne
Mexico City   Nairobi   Paris   Singapore
Taipei   Tokyo   Toronto

and associated companies in
Berlin   Ibadan

Copyright © 1996 by Carol Zaleski

Published by Oxford University Press, Inc.
198 Madison Avenue, New York, New York 10016

Library of Congress Cataloging–in–Publication Data
Zaleski, Carol.
Life of the world to come : near-death experience and Christian
hope : the Albert Cardinal Meyer lectures / Carol Zaleski.
p.   cm.
ISBN 0–19–510335–1
1. Near-death experiences—Religious aspects—Christianity.
2. Future life. I. Title.
BT902.Z35   1996   236'.2—dc20   95–23833

1 3 5 7 9 8 6 4 2

Printed in the United States of America
on acid-free paper

For Phil

Preface

The Life of the World to Come is an expanded version of three lectures I gave as the 1993 Albert Cardinal Meyer Lecturer at the University of St. Mary of the Lake/Mundelein Seminary.

The lectures took place in three sessions, over the course of a day-long symposium, on a Saturday within the Octave of Easter, April 17, 1993. In editing the lectures for publication I have retained my remarks about the day and the season in order to highlight the liturgical dimension of the Christian eschatological imagination. The lectures form a set of meditations on the three great hours (Lauds, Vespers, and Compline) of the Divine Office.

I am grateful to His Eminence Joseph Cardinal Bernardin; Very Rev. Gerald F. Kicanas, former Rector of Mundelein Seminary; and other members of the Lecture Committee for the invitation to give the Meyer Lectures; to Rev. Robert Barron for his hospitality during my stay at Mundelein Seminary; to the current Rector, Very Rev. John F. Canary, and many other faculty members and seminarians for their kindness; and especially to Rev. Andrew M. Greeley for his unfailing support.

Among those who read and commented on the manuscript, I am most grateful to Paul Burholt; Stratford and Léonie Caldecott; Dame Felicitas Corrigan, O.S.B.; Peggy Ellsberg; Paul J. Griffiths; Dame Gertrude Hughes, O.S.B.; and Dom Gregory Phillips, O.S.B. Whatever I may understand of Christian liturgical life I owe to the Benedictine communities in Petersham, Massachusetts: St. Scholastica Priory, led by Very Rev. Mother Mary Clare Vincent, O.S.B.; and St. Mary's Monastery, led by Rev. Dom Anselm Atkinson, O.S.B.; and also to Rt. Rev. Dom Hugh Gilbert, O.S.B., Abbot of Pluscarden Abbey in Scotland.

In preparing these lectures I was helped by research support from Smith College, research assistance from Lyn Harbaugh, and the efforts of the Inter-library Loan staff at Neilson Library, Smith College.

My son John, at the tender age of five, suggested several of the metaphysical reflections in these pages. My husband Philip Zaleski was a great help, as always. Finally, I'd like to thank Cynthia A. Read, Senior Editor at Oxford University Press, for a decade of encouragement and wise counsel.

Contents

The Life
of the
World to Come

ONE

Lauds

Awakening to the Reality of Death

This book is a meditation upon last things: the encounter with death, the hope for life beyond death, and the vision of the world to come, as distilled in the classical Christian tradition and recent testimony of near-death experience. As William James once defended the right to believe before all the evidence is in, I will defend the right to imagine a state of blessedness after death.

A *New Yorker* cartoon by Charles Addams shows two recent arrivals in heaven. One is saying to the other: "I knew about the wings, but the webbed feet are a surprise."[1] My argument will be that we have every right to fit ourselves in advance for a pair of wings as long as we recognize that such expectations are no proper measure of the surprise that awaits us.

All Christian hope flows from the Easter mystery of death and resurrection. By a happy accident, the lectures from which this book evolved took place during the Paschal season, on a day that

Western Christians celebrate as the first Saturday in Eastertide and Eastern Christians observe as Holy Saturday. On this day the Christian world is seemingly divided between celebrating the resurrection of Christ and mourning his death. It is a painful division, yet it may have something to teach us: that Christians are being asked to live simultaneously in the face of death and in the hope of resurrection.

In fact, the rites of the passion never simply replay what happened on the day that Jesus of Nazareth died; they are shot through with the awareness that his death was not the end. The very character of death has changed; life has intruded upon death. By the same token, the letter to the Hebrews insists that the resurrection cannot be understood apart from Christ's sacrifice. The resurrection does not cancel death, but transfigures it. As F. X. Durrwell puts it, the death of Christ is "inlaid in the life of glory," and our passage to that glory must go by way of death.[2] For St. Paul this coincidence of opposites is the indelible standard of Christian hope—by virtue of having a share in Christ's death, all shall be made alive.[3] If such abundant life is to be found in the death of Christ, and if his death has truly been taken up into his risen glory, then it is no scandal that the passion and the resurrection are commemorated on the same day. Both passion and resurrection can be celebrated—as indeed they are in the Eucharist—as one and the same action of divine love.

This book takes its structure and part of its theme from the Divine Office, which traces the mystery of death and resurrection through the course of a single day. A day is the miniature of a life and of an aeon. With its alternation of dawn and darkness, waking and rest, a day is a little cosmos, and we dwell within it as creatures of a day. The liturgy of the hours consecrates and interprets this daily round, finding in its natural rhythms a revealed meaning: the remembrance of creation and the anticipation of last things. Even a cursory review of the psalms, hymns, and antiphons with which the liturgy of the hours greets morning, evening, and night reveals a rich vein of eschatological memory and hope.

If one may speak of an eschatology proper to the Divine Office, the predominance of natural imagery—the imagery of darkness and light, sleep and waking—suggests that it consists in a poignant awareness of the presence of death in life and of life in death. To the great events of salvation history, upon which Christian hope hinges, the Divine Office weds the humble events of daily and nightly human and animal life. The Church wakes, hoping to watch with Christ, and the Church sleeps, hoping to rest in Christ. The sleeping and waking of the natural world is not extrinsic to this Christian hope but consecrated by it. The liturgy of the hours is echoed not only by the angels, but also by the fieldmice and sparrows; it is the chorus of creation.

In the Divine Office, Christian hope begins anew each day, facing death directly and at the same time facing East. The first light, sighted by the watchmen of dawn, is the morning star, symbol at once of Christ, Mary, and John the Baptist, "sent to bear witness to the light" (John 1:8). The Canticle of Zechariah sung at Lauds hails the newborn John as the forerunner to the light that is about to break forth upon "those who dwell in darkness and in the shadow of death" (Luke 1:68–79).

I am reminded of the practice among the Oglala Sioux of

gathering just before dawn, especially during times of crisis, to greet the morning star. In his 1931 interviews with poet John G. Neihardt, the Oglala holy man Black Elk recounted:

> I usually get up about the time the morning star rises and my people were to have knowledge from this star and people seemed all to know this. They were eager to see it come out and by the time the daybreak star came out the people would be saying, "Behold the star of wisdom."[4]

This practice was encouraged above all when there was a recent death in the community, for the daybreak star signified both illumination and regeneration.[5]

Lauds, similarly, is a communal service of awakening, praising the morning star of wisdom and rejoicing in the full sun whose light stirs the dead to life. One of the most ancient Christian morning hymns makes explicit the connections between greeting the dawn, being illumined by the risen Christ, and awakening from death: "Awake, O sleeper, and arise from the dead, and Christ shall give you light, the sun of the resurrection, begotten before the morning star, who gives life by his very own rays."[6]

Let us begin here, with this call to awaken from the sleep of death—a call that could easily be misconstrued. Are Christians being invited to think of themselves as immortal beings, invincible through identification with Christ the unconquered sun? Only an imperial Christianity could believe that. For Paul, who sings the same ancient hymn in Ephesians, it is a call to awaken from sin, to walk in light rather than darkness. Heedlessness,

7

inertia, spiritual deadness, these are the concern—not just the death that will rightfully claim each of us at the end of our days. Nor is the mere reassurance of survival after death sufficient to shake off the moral drowsiness that keeps us dead inside. Taken in isolation, the promise of an afterlife may even blunt our efforts to awaken from spiritual death. In order to awaken from death, we must first awaken to death.

Genuinely religious hope does not evade but rather consecrates that consciousness of death which is pivotal for the development of self-consciousness in human beings. Along with language (and intimately related to language), awareness of death uniquely marks our species. As soon as we could speak, we began to speak of death. And as soon as we could hear our words trail off into silence, we began to speak of realms beyond death.

Today, however, awareness of death has become acutely prob-lematic. The media saturate us with images of violent death, and a new illness—AIDS—conjures up memories of the *danse macabre* as it winds its way through rich and poor, the cultural elite and the dispossessed, carrying away children and men and women in their prime. At the same time, the ordinary experience of death in a family continues to be, in many communities of North America, suppressed or denied. As Ronald Blythe puts it "Everyone until recently knew the actual smell of death."[7] Death must be denied not because it is painful—it has always been painful—but because it signals the failure of our medical technology, the evaporation of our dream of progress and of individual self-fulfillment.

In this respect we are in an unprecedented situation. We have created two technologies with seemingly opposite functions: a medical and funeral technology that shields us from direct contact with death and an information and entertainment technology that bombards us with images of the deaths of strangers. The combined effect of these twin technologies can be almost comical. Consider, for instance, this full-page *New York Times* advertisement for the "Garden of Memories Non-Sectarian Mausoleums" in Paramus, New Jersey:

ABOVE-GROUND.
THE CLEAN BURIAL.
Not underground with earth's disturbing elements.
ACT NOW. AND GET 40% OFF.
Our fourth building almost completely sold.
Our fifth building (under construction) is selling fast.

MINIMIZE THE TRAUMA.
With death comes bitter grief, confusion and added responsibilities, at a time a family is least able to cope. Seeing a loved one being buried in the ground only adds to the stress. Above-ground burial helps alleviate some of the pain.

YOUR BURIAL. DON'T LET IT BE
A BURDEN TO YOUR FAMILY.
You can ease some of the burden by planning ahead. The choice is yours. Above-ground burial. The reasons are clear. It's clean, dry, civilized. Much less traumatic than below-ground burial.[8]

Here is a truly bizarre inverted dualism. Instead of protecting the earth from pollution by the decaying corpse, as the Zoroastrians do with their towers of silence, the above-ground mausoleums protect the corpse from pollution by the earth.

And if above ground isn't far enough removed from the disturbing, damp, uncivilized earth, there's an organization that offers burial in space. I quote from an advertisement in *New Age Journal:*

> It is now possible to have your cremated remains, or those of a loved one, placed aboard a rocket and sent to the sun where they will be transformed into pure energy, or sunshine, and radiated throughout the universe at the speed of light.
>
> Stellar Interment Corp. has negotiated the purchase of a rocket which will be licensed by the U.S. Department of State and which can be prepared for launch to the sun in approximately 3 years.
>
> Anyone can take part in this remarkable event by sending a minimum of one gram of ashes at the cost of $100 per gram to:
>
> **Stellar Interment Corp.**
>
> **575 University Blvd. East**
>
> **Silver Spring, MD 20901**
>
> any time before January 21st, 1989. The launch will be covered by the major news media.[9]

To my knowledge the launch has yet to occur. Our dead remain unprogressively earthbound. What is remarkable, though, is the way this advertisement resuscitates an archaic promise— that by assimilation to the sun a few chosen ones may escape the common fate of mortals. This is the promise made to the pharaohs of the Egyptian solar cult. But now it is democratized—"anyone can take part in this remarkable event"—within the limits of our market economy. One hundred dollars and a gram of ash are a small price to pay for the privilege of radiating throughout the universe at the speed of light.[10]

The compensatory function of these ways of thinking about death could not be more blatant. Can the same be said for every effort to envision life beyond death? Are they merely irrational stratagems to evade death or to make up for all that is lacking in life? No one can deny that human projections of life beyond death run counter to some rather obvious facts of experience. As Santayana once said, "The fact of being born augurs poorly for immortality."

Yet the realization that we are mortal is not so much a natural discovery as a gradual and imperfect acquisition of reason. As children, we find it more natural to imagine that we shall never die. Santayana writes:

Confidence in living for ever is anterior to the discovery that all men are mortal and to the discovery that the thinker is himself a man. These discoveries flatly contradict that confidence, in the form in which it originally presents itself, and all doctrines of immortality which adult philosophy can entertain are more or less subterfuges and after-thoughts by which the observed fact of mortality and the native inconceivability of death are more or less clumsily reconciled.[11]

The Freudian axiom, to which many continue to subscribe even in this post-Freudian age, is that the ego cannot tolerate the thought of its own death. As Freud put it in his 1915 essay "Thoughts for the Times on War and Death":

Our own death is indeed unimaginable, and whenever we make the attempt to imagine it we can perceive that we really survive as spectators. Hence the psychoanalytic school could venture on the assertion that at bottom no one believes in his own death, or to put the same thing in another way, in the unconscious every one of us is convinced of his own immortality.[12]

Thus the will to believe in immortality is easily reduced to a will to deceive oneself about death, and from this self-deception arises the whole fantastic panoply of compensatory paradises invented by the world's religions.

Like most of Freud's theories about the genesis of religion, this one is speculatively ingenious but historically unfounded. In their formative periods, none of the world's religions has exhibited elaborate conceptions of life after death. John Bowker's eloquent book *The Meanings of Death* makes this observation the basis for rejecting the crude analysis that would derive religions from the need for a compensatory afterlife; he then proposes a profound Christological interpretation in which sacrifice, rather than self-defense, provides the key to unlock the meanings of death.[13] It is a brilliant study; I hope, therefore, that he would agree with the friendly amendment I propose: that imaginatively rich conceptions of the future life may coexist with a genuinely sacrificial willingness to face death.

While the lack of articulated doctrines of the future life in the formative period of the enduring religious traditions offers protection against crude reductionist explanations, it is not sufficient grounds for considering that articulation deviant when it does occur. Unfortunately, this has been the premise behind recent efforts (most famously by Oscar Cullman) to strip away the language of immortality in order to restore the Christian eschatological imagination to its biblical purity.[14] The effect of this purifying critique has been to make many thoughtful Christians feel trapped in a forced choice between immortality of the soul and resurrection of the dead, between death as friend and death as enemy, between personal and collective forms of eschatological hope.[15]

What the critics of immortality language fail to grasp is the principle of "development of doctrine" in eschatology. Worse, they are simply tone-deaf when it comes to appreciating the varieties of the eschatological imagination. What they gain in consistency, they lose by cutting Christian eschatology off from its imaginative roots, from its links to the past, and from its relevance to popular religious longings.

The critics of immortality language in Christianity often cite as supporting evidence the lack of an articulated conception of an afterlife in the formative stages of biblical faith. But this lack should not be interpreted as equivalent to a skeptic's rejection of an already established doctrine of immortality. Strange as it may seem, it is common to find combined in one tradition emphatic statements of human mortality (as in the memorable verse from the Epic of Gilgamesh: "Gilgamesh, whither rovest thou? When the gods created mankind, Death for mankind they set aside, Life in their own hands retaining"[16]) and an abundance of folk practices and lore about ghosts, spirits, and journeys to other worlds.

Moreover, in traditional societies that possess a less individualistic ethos than our own, to speak of living on in communal memory, through one's accomplishments or through one's off-spring, is actually to say a great deal about transcendence of death. Historically, this simple and universal idea has often provided the germ for the elaboration of doctrines and symbols of immortality.

Examples of development of doctrine concerning life after death can be found not only in religious traditions but also in philosophical movements. In Spartan elegies, the term "immortal" or "deathless" (*athanatos*) is an honorific designation by which the poet and the *polis* could pledge eternal memory to their fallen defenders. This sounds rather like our empty use of "immortal" to refer to anyone famous who dies, as in "the immortal Babe Ruth." But it foreshadows the development of the Greek philosophical idea of the immortal soul and of philosophy as the supreme art of soul tending. Today, when "immortal" is used to mean merely celebrated, what we are witnessing is not the germ of a new idea but merely the leavings of a doctrine that has gone to seed, and that makes all the difference.

There is a danger of imposing artificial evolutionary schemes; nonetheless, unless we recognize that a similar development from germ to later flowerings can be traced in the biblical tradition, we will not be able to make intelligible the many kinds of eschatological thinking that arose in post-exilic Judaism, let alone in Christianity. It is no longer acceptable to assert that early Judaism lacked a notion of immortality; better to say that they left immortality in God's hands, never daring to assert that the human being possesses it by rights, and yet daring to hope that God would bestow a share in eternal life upon those who belong to him.

John J. Collins brings this point home with respect to the apocalyptic eschatology of post-exilic Judaism:

> the future hope of late post-exilic Judaism cannot be understood as the expectation of a purely future event, and, despite the etymology of the word eschatology, it is not primarily concerned with the end of anything. Rather it is concerned with the transcendence of death by the attainment of a higher, angelic form of life. This hope shows considerable affinities with the Greek doctrine of the immortality of the soul.[17]

Similarly, historical studies of early Christian and patristic eschatology reveal the remarkable complexity of Christian hope and resist simplistic polarizations of the tradition into biblical (or "Hebraic") versus Hellenic outlooks.[18] The wealth of historical material now accessible even to general readers should be enough to put to rest the uncritical assumption that immortality language entails rejection of biblical anthropology or evasion of the sting of death.

To speak more generally, if it is true, as the moral critiques of death denial assert, that traditional societies have done a better job than our own of coming to terms with death, then this also gives the lie to the modern conceit that belief in life after death is an evasion of the reality of death. There is no evidence that belief in an afterlife has functioned to block out awareness of death.

On the contrary, along with their variegated unfolding of conceptions of the afterlife, the world's religions have universally counseled humankind to keep death in mind, to keep death real.

"What man shall live and not see death?" asks the Psalmist.[19] "For the born, there is no such thing as not dying" is the reminder delivered by the Samyutta Nikāya of the Buddhist Pali canon.[20] "Every soul shall taste of death," warns the Qur'ān.[21] The metaphor of tasting is significant. Not only are we to see death, but to taste it, to take it into ourselves. The consolation of faith in life beyond death does not distance us from death, but gives us a means of facing death—our own and that of others— without despair.

The methodical cultivation of awareness of one's own death is a hallmark of spiritual practice, especially in traditions with a strong monastic culture. The *Rule* of St. Benedict, taking up a motif found pervasively in the *Apophthegmata patrum* and other records of the sayings and lives of the desert fathers, includes among the "tools for good works" the resolve "to hold death before one's eyes daily" ("mortem cotidie ante oculos suspectam habere").[22] So, too, Buddhist monastic literature abounds with exhortations to remember death, seeing this as a most effective way to develop compassion for all living beings and to progress toward full awakening. Among the samurai of feudal Japan remembrance of death was crucial to martial discipline. The seventeenth-century samurai Daidōji Yūzan Shigesuki makes this the central theme of his warrior code:

> One who is a samurai must before all things keep constantly in mind, by day and by night, from the time he takes up his chopsticks to eat his New Year's breakfast to Old Year's night when he pays his yearly bills, the fact that he has to die. That is his chief business.[23]

For the Stoics and their twentieth-century children, the Existentialists, awareness of death is the key to wisdom and self-possession. Today the "death awareness" movement associated with the work of Elisabeth Kübler-Ross has taken up the same theme, proclaiming that full awareness of death will fix everything that is wrong with our psyches and our civilization. But caution is in order here. Denial of death is a more complex psychological and social phenomenon than the death-awareness movement seems to allow.

Moreover, what it would mean to stop denying death is not altogether clear. The cultivation of awareness of death is not a simple unblinkering of human reason but a complex spiritual discipline, which serves different aims for Epictetus than for Benedict, or Śāntideva, or Heidegger. Since death is the defining limit against which we measure the aim of human life, a call to remembrance of death can mean almost anything: seize the day, gather your roses, make ready for battle, repent of your sins, realize your impermanence and interdependence on all sentient beings, abide in the peaceable kingdom of the present moment. The implications of death awareness are as various as the definitions of the good life.

Awareness of death is also ineradicably an imaginative activity. Wherever there is a vacuum—an unknown to be contemplated—images rush in. Death may be imagined as a person, for example. Stories are told in every culture of how death came into the world, by an act of disobedience or, more often, a cosmic blunder. Even if we like to believe we have outgrown such mythic thinking, it is embedded in our language; for instance, we say of someone who died that "he met his death."

Whether we think of death as a dark void or as the doorway to another life, we are engaging in imagistic thinking. By what criteria, then, shall we determine which kinds of imagistic thinking are sound? As an exercise in asking this question, let us consider near-death experience.[24]

Near-death experience first received widespread attention in 1975 with the publication of *Life After Life* by Raymond Moody.[25] A former philosophy professor turned psychiatrist, Moody began collecting stories of near-death experience while still in medical school. On the basis of 150 reports, Moody arrived at a description of the typical near-death experience which quickly became the standard source for portrayal of death and its aftermath in films and other popular media.

Moody's book inspired several ambitious clinical studies. The subject continues to receive attention, not only in the media but also in journals of psychology and medicine, and in the publications of professional societies for near-death studies in the United States, the United Kingdom, France, Norway, Holland, and Australia.[26]

In a 1981 Gallup survey, 15 percent of the U.S. sample reported having had a close brush with death. Of that number 34 percent claimed that the episode triggered ecstatic or visionary states of consciousness.[27] What really accounts for the appeal of near-death testimony is not its frequency, however, but the compelling quality of the anecdotal accounts. Neither the clinical studies nor the survey results can match the impact of hearing firsthand narrative testimony from survivors who have evidently been transfigured by a close brush with death. It is tempting, therefore, to construct a master narrative, drawing upon diverse accounts, as Moody has done.[28]

The following features recur throughout contemporary accounts:

1. Separation from the body, sometimes accompanied by a "spectator" perspective, watching the scene of crisis from a distant or elevated vantage point.

2. Journey motifs, such as drifting through darkness, outer space, a "void," or a tunnel.

3. Encounter with deceased relatives or friends, or with a godlike or angelic presence (Moody's "being of light").

4. Review of one's past deeds in the form of a panoramic visual replay of memories (the life review). In cases of sudden encounter with life-threatening danger, this life review often takes precedence over other features.

5. Immersion in light and love. Many confess that this experience is indescribable. Cognitive and affective characteristics are fused. The keynote is a profound sense of security and protection, accompanied by a sense of receiving special messages or hidden truths. For some, this takes the form of an instantaneous, timeless, and comprehensive vision of the totality of existence.

6. Return to life, either involuntarily or by choice, to complete unfinished business on earth.

7. Transforming aftereffects, such as loss of fear of death, newfound zest for everyday life, and renewed dedication to the values of empathetic love, lifelong learning, and service to others. For some, these positive effects are accompanied by difficulties in adjusting to normal life.

The first reports on near-death experience in the media presented this testimony as exciting new evidence for an afterlife. In an effort to stem the tide of sensationalism, experts came forward from several quarters eager to attribute near-death experience to the mind-altering effects of drugs and anesthetics or to conditions that are part of the normal physiology of dying, such as oxygen deprivation, sensory isolation, elevated endorphin levels, and seizure activity in the brain. Near-death testimony was added to the list of targets (along with metal bending and trance channeling) for debunking attacks by members of the Committee for Scientific Investigation of Claims of the Paranormal, a group of crusading skeptics.[29]

What both critics and researchers failed to notice was the striking evidence for the cultural shaping of near-death experience. They were unaware that what we call near-death experience today is nothing new. Stories of people who return from death, bringing back eyewitness testimony about the other world, can be found in nearly every religious tradition, and although they have many similar features, such reports invariably portray this experience in ways that conform to cultural expectations. Had the critics realized this, they no doubt would have added it to their arsenal of arguments against the veridicality of near-death experience.[30]

What are we to make of this testimony? None of the responsible researchers would claim that it is proof of an afterlife. This should not prevent us from taking it seriously, however. The final meaning of a near-death experience can never be exhaustively accounted for merely by taking an inventory of the physiological, psychological, and cultural conditions that shape it.

At the risk of sounding cryptic, I would like to suggest that near-death experience is at once imaginative and real. It is a real experience mediated by the religious imagination. It is an imaginative encounter with death and a symbolic crossing of the threshold of death. Across that threshold lies the other world, which for our present purposes can be understood as the realm of the imagination, a realm in which the ideals that animate this life are encountered in their fullest, most embodied form.

The other world, in this sense, is the inner world, where I meet myself and read the story of my life. Although I hasten to add that the reality of the other world exceeds the imagination, in the present life this reality is met only by means of imaginative forms. Hence if near-death experience is to be considered something more than mere illusion, it must be acknowledged to be at once imaginative and real.

In addition, near-death experience can be classed among conversion experiences, in which the subject undergoes a symbolic death and rebirth. As such, it deserves to be evaluated in the way that William James suggests, by attending to its "fruits for life," its overall meaning and effects on the subject's life.

The fruits of a near-death experience can be loss of fear of death, newfound appreciation for life, and rededication to one's highest ideals. These fruits can be passed along to others who hear of the near-death experience and are thereby touched or consoled. Near-death stories may prove nothing about human prospects for continued existence after death, but they do provide, at the least, a narrative pledge that our animating values have an enduring reality which is not going to be taken away by death.

New questions arise, however, when we try to draw out the possible connections between the phenomena of near-death experience and the traditional features of Christian eschatology. Far from providing unambiguous confirmation of Christian hope, near-death testimony poses some real problems for Christian eschatological thinking. The problems can be described briefly as follows:

1. Since near-death experience often can be explained naturalistically, it is not a secure place on which to pin one's hopes.

2. If we decide that near-death experience is veridical, then we have to face a more serious difficulty. Taken as empirical evidence of an afterlife, near-death testimony appears to make revelation irrelevant. If we have at our disposal natural sources of information about such mysteries, then what need have we for revealed promises? If we possess immortality as our natural birthright, then what need have we for a redeemer to conquer death?

3. Contemporary accounts of near-death experience are pervaded by a saccharine optimism about death, radically different from the complex, even bittersweet, character of Christian hope.

What then can near-death experience teach us about Christian hope? At the very least, it gives us a glimpse into the workings of the eschatological imagination, the primary vehicle for that hope. We must give further consideration to the bearing of near-death experience on the question of the right to believe in, and the right to imagine, individual survival after death. The relationship of this question to specifically Christian hope will be our chief concern in the next chapter.

Vespers

Experiences at the Threshold of Death—
Intimations of Immortality?

At Vespers, under the sign of the evening star, the Church gathers in the harvest of the day, expressing thanks for its fruitfulness. Vespers marks the beginning of the end of the day, of the *saeculum* in miniature. It is a first sighting of night, a time of prayer for the dead and anticipation of the life of the world to come.

Near-death experience has a vesperal quality. It is a first sighting of death rather than a direct experience of it; it is a visionary anticipation, mediated by the images of death and beyond that are engraved on one's psyche and embedded in one's culture. By itself, near-death testimony does not provide objective evidence for an afterlife, yet I will contend that it is something more than a mere grab bag of subjective experiences irrelevant to Christian hope.

We should begin by reiterating that near-death experience is nothing new. Near-death reports are common in shamanic cul-

tures, for example; often it is by means of a visionary experience of death and rebirth (an experience whose basic features are well known in advance) that the shaman is initiated and endowed with the power to heal, the gift of vision, the knowledge to assist the hunt, and the authority to serve as custodian of sacred lore.[1] Today's near-death reports show a similar initiatory pattern, but for lack of a supporting culture they remain comparatively private and idiosyncratic.

Striking analogues can be found as well in the Jewish, Christian, and Islamic accounts of prophets, saints, and sages who journeyed to the other world, ascended to the divine throne, or toured the regions of heaven and hell, thereby receiving special knowledge and authorization to preach or prophesy: Enoch, St. Paul, and Muhammad are only the most famous examples.[2] Again, although the near-death experience is structurally similar, it lacks the authoritative character of a communally sanctioned prophetic or apocalyptic testament.

Dramatic accounts of souls traveling beyond the body are a common feature of the archaic and classical cultures of the Mediterranean world, even in the absence of articulated doctrines of the afterlife. The literary motif of the journey beyond the body is undoubtedly linked to pervasive folk belief in a free soul that ventures abroad during sleep, trance, death, and ecstasy, or even during momentary fits of abstraction such as a yawn or a sneeze.[3]

The Greco-Roman mysteries, for all their extraordinary variety, brought to common beliefs about the free soul a more organized narrative and ritual structure and set in motion a complex process by which the adventures of the free soul came to be linked to the personal experience of salvation, transformative knowledge, and victory over death.

The Eleusinian mysteries, for example, celebrated the myth of Demeter and Persephone with a graded series of initiatory dramas that mimic death and rebirth. Step by step, the initiand was led from darkness toward the exalted state called *epopteia,* direct vision of the light. To become one of the beholders of the light was to pass irrevocably from death to life. The seventh-century B.C. Eleusinian text known as the *Homeric Hymn to Demeter* extols the beatific character of that vision: "Happy is he among men upon earth who has seen these mysteries! But he who is uninitiate and who has no part in them, never has lot of like good things once he is dead, down in the darkness and gloom."[4] The mysteries provided a theater for mimetic encounter with death; by the same token, they offered a way of interpreting death in theatrical and initiatory terms.

A passage attributed to Plutarch describes the *psychē's* experience of death as the same as the experience of those being initiated in the great mysteries.[5] The word for initiation, *teleisthai,* Plutarch remarks, is similar to the word for dying, *teleutan;* both are forms of consummation, *telos.* Both experiences begin in fear and darkness and end in light and blessedness:

> At first there is wandering, and wearisome roaming, and fearful traveling through darkness with no end to be found. Then, just before the consummation [*telos*], there is every sort of terror, shuddering and trembling and perspiring and being alarmed. But after this a marvelous light [*phos*] appears, and open places

and meadows await, with voices and dances and the solemnities of sacred utterances and holy visions. In that place one walks about at will, now perfect and initiated [*memuemenos*] and free, and wearing a crown, one celebrates religious rites, and joins with pure and pious people. Such a person looks over the uninitiated and unpurified crowd of people living here, who are packed together and trample each other in deep mud and murk, but who hold onto their evil things on account of their fear of death, because they do not believe in the good things that are in the other world.[6]

Death is the ultimate initiation, Plutarch suggests; yet the initiate who meets death will possess the incomparable advantage of having rehearsed for the final drama. Similarly, Clement of Alexandria quotes Pindar as saying, "Blessed is the one who goes under the earth after seeing these things. That person knows the end of life, and knows its Zeus-given beginning."[7]

That there was a free *psychē* was commonly assumed by ancient Greek thinkers; but that the adventures of the free *psychē* might be linked to the acquisition of saving knowledge and the *metanoia* of the whole person was a novel idea. Only gradually did a conception of the *psychē* as a unitary soul, endowed with ethical and psychological characteristics and functioning as the center of consciousness, emerge in the philosophical and religious literature of ancient Greece. Once this occurred, it became possible for philosophers to appropriate the archaic imagery of the soul journey and read back into the mysteries an explicit ethical and eschatological doctrine. Hellenistic Jewish and Christian thinkers like Philo and Clement of Alexandria were consequently able to see the ancient mysteries not merely as demonic inversions but as profound anticipations of their own traditions. Above all, it was the Platonic allegorization of the mysteries that made this interpretation possible.

In the *Phaedo,* Plato borrows the motif of the soul's initiatory rehearsal for death from unnamed Orphic and Pythagorean sources and makes it into an allegory for the philosophic life. The philosopher's task is to prepare for death, and the best preparation is to be "half dead" already—that is, to turn the mind's gaze toward what is enduringly true, good, and beautiful. By this *metanoia,* the philosopher becomes personally identified with the changeless reality which can never admit of any mixture of death.

To a great extent it is Plato's imagery rather than his doctrine that has recommended him to succeeding generations of religious thinkers. What made the Platonic legacy so attractive to Christian philosophers like Augustine and Gregory of Nyssa was the dramatic picture it offered of the dynamics of the soul's conversion. Oscar Cullman's charge that "I Corinthians 15 has been sacrificed for the *Phaedo*" completely misses this point.[8] The allegory of the cave and the sun, the story of our life in the hollows of the earth, the image of the winged chariot, the myths of memory and forgetting—all are imagistic ways of evoking intimations of a wider life and longings for forgotten truths.

These are precisely the kinds of moods and longings that are expressed, though admittedly with less artistry, by contemporary near-death reports. The accounts often have a strangely Platonic flavor. One woman, whose brush with death occurred during childbirth, has related an experience very like a mystical *anāmnesis*.[9] Finding herself in a shimmering green meadow adorned with flowers, fragrance, and light (reminiscent of the classical and medieval *locus amoenus*), she was met by four robed guides who granted her the privilege of asking three questions. "Can you tell me what everything is all about?" she asked. The answer came to her in just a few sentences, but they seemed to comprise everything; all at once she was given a comprehensive vision of the whole, and she found herself assenting to that vision with her entire being, saying: "Ah, yes, this is what I always knew, how could I have forgotten?"

When the summons came for her to return to life, she was told that she would not be allowed to take back with her the memory of those few sentences. In effect, she was forced to drink the waters of Lethe. To this day, she has a lingering sense of having been given a glimpse of the whole, and it causes her no little frustration that she cannot remember it.

The testimony of near-death experience, like the literature of mystical experience in general, abounds in such interrupted visions. The man from Porlock invariably breaks in; the visionary finds herself, upon awakening, unable to retrieve—whether for private reflection or public disclosure—the details of her vision. So Dante tells it in the final Canto of the *Paradiso:* the visionary is given to see, in the very living light of truth, the universal form in which all substance and accidents are fused by love—but a moment later, he lapses into forgetfulness. Although the specific content of the revelation is forgotten, however, a magnetic memory of it is retained—one senses when one is moving in its direction—and this may be sufficient to reset the heart's compass.

Medieval Christian Return-from-Death Stories

The closest analogues in Christian tradition to modern near-death reports are the medieval stories of men and women who die, visit purgatory, hell, and heaven, and then return to life.[10] Like today's accounts, they feature ordinary people rather than prophets, shamans, or sages; they are stories of personal transformation, and they serve some obvious didactic aims.

Several influential return-from-death stories appear in the *Dialogues* of Gregory the Great, the sixth-century pope and spiritual writer.[11] In the last book of the *Dialogues,* which treats of miracles surrounding death, we meet a hermit who died and went to hell, was sent back to mend his ways, and spent the rest of his life performing penances and austerities; a merchant who returned to life after it was discovered that he had been summoned to death by mistake, having been confused with a blacksmith of the same name; a soldier who died in the terrible plague of 584 and returned to life with an eyewitness account of a purgatorial test bridge. These stories are intended to provide, as encouragement to the weak, clear proof of the immortality of the soul, the reality of postmortem punishment, and the efficacy of the Church's penitential and intercessory practices.

In the eighth century, the Venerable Bede included in his *Ecclesiastical History of the English People* an influential tale of an ordinary Northumbrian family man who died and returned to life, interrupting the last rites and terrifying his poor wife by springing bolt upright on his deathbed.[12] He claimed to have been met by a "man of shining countenance and bright apparel" who escorted him to a purgatorial valley of flame and ice and from thence to the pit of hell, where he saw malign spirits carrying off the souls of a priest, a layman, and a woman. After narrowly escaping the demons' tongs, he traveled with his guide in a southeasterly direction to the flowery meadows of paradise, which he mistook at first for heaven. At the end of the journey, he was given a brief taste of the fragrance, light, and bliss of the heavenly kingdom. Sent back to life against his will, his sole aim was to retrace his steps back to heaven. Telling his wife that "from now on, I must no longer live according to my old habits," he distributed his property, entered a monastery, and undertook the corrective regimen of bathing every day in an icy stream. Bede comments that the spiritual transformation of the protagonist is an even more impressive miracle than his return from death.

This account was one of the models for a series of extended narratives, mostly of monastic provenance, describing ordinary folk who died, traveled to purgatory, hell, and heaven, and returned transformed. The heyday of such narratives was the twelfth century. Dante, who was familiar with the tradition, used it as raw material for his masterpiece.

There are some remarkable similarities between medieval Christian return-from-death narratives and contemporary accounts of near-death experience. A template for the story would look something like this: The visionary leaves his body, looking back at it with the disinterested glance of a spectator; he is met by a luminous being who serves as his guide; he witnesses a visual replay of his past deeds, weighing them against an inner standard of right and wrong. Escorted to heavenly realms (flowery meadows, gardens, luminous cities), he is given a brief taste of the supernal delights that are the reward of the blessed. The experience is said to be indescribable—yet it is described, nonetheless, in shimmering and synaesthetic detail, as an immersion in light and love, bringing with it both ecstatic joy and intuitive knowledge. The visionary longs to remain caught up in this heavenly state, but is sent back to life. Upon returning to life, he is permanently transformed. Initially reticent, he is persuaded to tell his story for the sake of its didactic and consoling effect on others. The story is told and retold, and reshaped in the retelling, in sermons and chronicles, in scholarly treatises and across backyard fences.

There are many more similarities than I have managed to convey in this brief summary, but there are significant differences as well. Most striking, of course, is the absence from most twentieth-century near-death accounts of postmortem punishment: no hell, no purgatory, no chastening torments or telltale agonies at the moment of death. The life review, when it occurs, is a reassuring experience, modeled on contemporary methods of education and psychotherapy.

The guide figure is often a family member or a generic spiritual presence, and is always friendly and comforting. In the medieval accounts the guide is usually a guardian angel or patron saint, who for the sake of the visionary's eventual salvation is not above dangling his charge over the pit of hell. The possibility for loss is genuine in the medieval accounts—if one botches the second chance, eternal damnation is the likely result. Today it seems that there is scarcely any possibility for loss. Life and afterlife flow together as an unending stream of fresh opportunities for personal growth.

What of the transforming effects of the near-death experience? Today they take the form of freedom from everyday worries and from fear of death, poignant appreciation for the ordinary moments of life, and passionate dedication to the values of love, learning, and service. The social expression of these values varies greatly. Medieval accounts have a more penitential theme, and expect the visionary to express his transformed state of mind in a sanctioned institutional form, for example, as a pilgrim or monk.

The similarities suggest that there are some enduring—perhaps even universal—features of near-death experience. The differences make it clear, however, that near-death experiences, and the literature that describes them, are profoundly shaped by cultural expectations. The researchers have been naive about this point, claiming that the lack of what they call "traditional" features (St. Peter at the gate or demons with pitchforks) is a sign of freedom from mythology.

At this point, we totter perilously close to the edge of dismissing near-death testimony as "nothing but" a projection of cultural values, wishes, and norms. Only a lively appreciation for the revelatory potential of the religious imagination can keep us from falling over that edge into the fold of the skeptics and debunkers. That is a cheerless prospect, so let me try now to rally our forces. I maintain that a full admission of the imaginative character of otherworld visions provides the most secure defense of the right to believe in such experiences.

A near-death experiencer is certain that he was dead; the experts say no. I say yes, in a way; it was a visionary encounter with death. The visionary "met his death" (note that this phrase retains a vestige of the image of death as a person). In that symbolic encounter, the visionary entered the other world—that is, the domain of the imagination, the inner world turned inside out and projected on the stage of imagination. On this stage the drama of life and death, judgment and redemption, is acted out.

The problem with this approach is that people still ask me, "Yes, but what do you *really* think is going on?" By stressing the symbolic and imaginative character of near-death experience, have we really protected it from reductionist analysis?

A great deal depends upon how one understands symbol. Not so long ago, a symbol was seen as a mask that embellishes or conceals an idea that might otherwise be expressed in straightforward moral or religious terms. More recently, however—thanks to the influence of such philosophers and theologians as Paul Tillich, Ernst Cassirer, Susanne Langer, Paul Ricoeur, and David Tracy—the symbol has been interpreted as a mediating form by which realities are conveyed that are not available for conceptual expression. A living symbol participates in the reality it represents. It does not copy or fully contain that reality, but it does communicate some of its power.

To answer the question, "What do I *really* think?" requires moving from such general reflections to a concrete religious stance. What I *really* think, then, is that the God of Abraham,

Isaac, and Jacob is at once a God who declares, "No one shall see me and live,"[13] and a God who wishes to be known. To show himself directly would be to destroy our freedom, not to mention our nerves. Kierkegaard has expressed this point unforgettably in his parable of the king and the maiden in the *Philosophical Fragments:* how can the king reveal his love to the humble maiden without overwhelming and indeed crushing her nature? The king's dilemma is this: "Not to reveal oneself is the death of love, to reveal oneself is the death of the beloved!"[14] The king's only recourse is to court the maiden indirectly, by descending to her, taking on the form of a servant. And the form of the servant must be no mere disguise: the king must really become the servant.

Following this analogy, we may ask, If God, the unknowable, wishes to be known, what other recourse does God have but to avail himself of our images and symbols, just as he has availed himself of our flesh? St. Ephrem the Syrian made this suggestion in one of his hymns *On Faith:* "He clothed Himself in language, so that He might clothe us in His mode of life."[15]

If God is willing to descend into our human condition, may he not also, by the same courtesy, descend into our cultural forms and become mediated to us in and through them? To deny that this courteous descent can take place is to reinvent the heresy of the iconoclasts.

Such a *katābasis* would transfigure our all-too-human forms, so that they no longer serve merely self-serving ends; this is one test of a genuine religious symbol. But no matter how genuine, the symbol can never become completely transparent to the reality it represents. We cannot know what awaits us after death, but we can legitimately believe all that our tradition teaches and our experience suggests. We believe all this under correction; and—if we love a good surprise—we look forward to the correction.

The truth about eschatology is itself eschatological. Now we see in an enigma darkly, in the mirror of our culture. Only "then," when the veil is lifted, shall we see face to face. Now we must test the soundness of our images and symbols by practicing the traditional and modern arts of discernment, guided by both dogma and experience. Only then shall we know as we are known.

The Right to Believe

But what of the question, Are we rationally and morally entitled to believe in life after death? Death has become so fearsome today, so "wild," as Philippe Ariès puts it, that a tremendous apologetic burden has been placed on arguments for immortality.

F. W. H. Myers, the classics scholar, psychical researcher, and friend of William James, once said that the most important of all questions was, "Is the Universe friendly?" The answer, he believed, depended upon whether one could succeed in demonstrating empirically the survival of human consciousness after death. Like many British and American intellectuals who were caught up in the spiritualist movement at the turn of the century, Myers had hopes of placing the wish to survive death on scientific footing. The charge of wishful thinking is fairly compelling in this case, especially since the notion of surviving death carried with it no dread of being judged.

Similarly, those who flock to buy books on near-death experience want to hear that they will not be robbed of the satisfaction of continued personal existence; they do not want to hear that they will be held accountable for sins. Studies conducted by Andrew M. Greeley and his colleagues at the National Opinion Research Center and the International Social Survey Program indicate that people (indeed, the overwhelming majority of those surveyed) believe in life after death above all because they believe that they are loved.

Only with the decline of belief in hell has the search for proofs of life after death become such an attractive pastime. John Henry Newman, in contrast, took it for granted that any successful philosophical argument for immortality would automatically bring with it overpowering fear and trembling, and desire to repent.[16] A similar transformation has taken place with respect to the classical Indian doctrine of *samsāra* (rebirth). Especially in its recent imported forms, the doctrine of rebirth has come to be seen as the consoling promise of many lifetimes. In its classical forms, however, it described a sorrowful state of human bondage within which, impelled by one's own karma, one must undergo an endless series of judgment days.

Christian hope—in this respect like classical Hindu and Buddhist hope—is more complex than a mere promise of survival. If the question is about immortality, then, as Jaroslav Pelikan has expressed it, "The Christian answer . . . is both yes and no."[17] It is not as though the problem of life is solved by the promise of life after death. If anything, life becomes more problematic, more mysterious, less under control, when interpreted by Christian hope.

The Christian attitude toward death is like Joseph's attitude toward his treacherous brothers: "Even though you intended to harm me, God intended it for good" (Gen. 50:20).[18] Death intends our harm, yet God converts that harm to good. From the Christian viewpoint, this conversion occurs when one identifies with the sacrificial death of Christ and is thereby raised to new life in Christ.

Is this wishful thinking? If so, it is a very complex wish, not yielding the kind of immediate gratification offered by spiritualist eschatologies. If Christian hope involves wishful thinking, it also entails the considerable risk of astonishment in the event that the wish comes true. One danger of wishful thinking is that one may get what one wishes—fulfillment never comes in the form one expects. The history of Jewish and Christian eschatology is a history of the overturning of expectations—messianic expectations, in particular—without the falsifying of the underlying wish.

Considering how radically we are changed by every critical crossing of the stream of life, it stands to reason that the translation to eternal life must be far more wonderful and more terrible than anything we have dared to wish. But it must also exact a correspondingly higher price. We pay not just with our flesh (a fair bargain, since its value depreciates with age) but with the very surrender of ourselves. As John Bowker puts it, "We owe both God and entropy a death."[19]

It seems likely that the narrow ego-self, whose fear of extinction was said to be the source of conceptions of eternal life, will not survive the translation to eternal life intact. Afterlife scenarios in which the ego and its possessions do survive intact have a comic effect. These are the scenarios that are most obviously shaped by transient cultural preoccupations and psychological needs. When we consider the banal domestic vision of heaven—complete with smoking jacket and golden retriever—found in *Gates Ajar* and similar works of Victorian consolation literature, or the gauzy beings who cavort in the pastures of the spiritualist Summerland, we can appreciate Thoreau's remark that he would gladly trade his immortality for a glass of cold beer.

We know that our strongest wishes and desires cloud our judgment; it is therefore sensible to be cautious about indulging them. There is a nobility to the heroic realism and ascetic rationality of the Freudian tradition. We should be suspicious of any easy confidence in immortality.

On the other hand, we also know that our strongest wishes and desires reveal to us a world of meaning and possibilities to which a premature skepticism would block our access. We may be justified, then, in wagering on them. We may make an argument from desire, on the premise that some desires have the power not merely to tint but to transfigure our common experience, bringing about an objective change in our world. According to Miguel de Unamuno, the great Spanish philosopher-poet, we owe it to our humanity not to stifle the desire for immortality:

> We must needs believe in the other life, in the eternal life beyond the grave, and in an individual and personal life, in a life in which each one of us may feel his consciousness and feel that it is united, without being confounded, with all other consciousnesses in the Supreme Consciousness, in God; we must needs believe in

that other life in order that we may live this life, and endure it, and give it meaning and finality. And we must needs believe in that other life, perhaps, in order that we may deserve it, in order that we may obtain it, for it may be that he neither deserves it nor will obtain it who does not passionately desire it above reason and, if need be, against reason.[20]

This view sounds extreme, but perhaps it will seem less so if we consider an example from the sphere of ordinary human affections. I love you, therefore I think that you love me. Perhaps I am not accurately reading your feelings, but merely projecting upon you, my hapless chosen victim, my own wish to be loved. Nonetheless, you are affected, and you respond. You are persuaded by my argument from desire. You love me back. My love for you was in any case an early detection of your potential to respond to me with love. If I were to short-circuit this process by skepticism about wishful thinking, then yes, it would all end right here. The romance would be finished before it had a chance to begin, and the suspicion would be confirmed that romantic love is an illusion, a mere cultural construction masking a biological imperative. The very face of the world would be changed.

It will be argued, of course, that the mere wish for another life, however strongly felt, is not capable of changing the implacable laws of our universe. And there is no lasting comfort in taking refuge in mere credulity. Indulging a wish against reason to continue life beyond death begins to look cowardly and ignoble. Can there be, then, an argument from desire to support the hope for eternal life?

We have an indelible desire for those whom we love to be preserved in God's love. Therefore, we think, it must be true; we will it to be true; we live as if it were true; we wager on its truth. And we receive an advance on the wager's earnings, in the form of hope. William James has argued that the will to believe, in such a case, is not counter-rational. When a question of existential urgency presents itself, we cannot wait for all the evidence to come in: we must decide. It is not a matter of passion overcoming reason, as Unamuno would have it. Rather, it is reasonable to reach beyond what our immediate knowledge can demonstrate, to postulate eternal life (to use the Kantian term) and also to imagine it, in order to orient ourselves in the present life. Our passion has a contribution to make which it would be positively irrational to rule out.

Another face of the argument from desire emerges when we witness extreme suffering. Rationalistic theodicies inevitably break down in the face of extreme suffering; Job's comforters are resoundingly rebuked. The attempt to justify God's ways to man is rightly discredited for its shallowness and impiety. Nonetheless, at the risk of indulging in compensatory fantasies, one may venture to hope that God will set things right in a future life. Cardinal Newman makes this point by quoting from a popular story the words of a dying factory girl:

> I think if this should be the end of all, and if all I have been born for is just to work my heart and life away, and to sicken in this dree place, with those millstones in my ears for ever, until I could scream out for them to stop and let me have a little piece of

quiet, and with the fluff filling my lungs, until I thirst to death
for one long deep breath of the clear air, and my mother gone,
and I never able to tell her again how I loved her, and of all my
troubles,—I think, if this life is the end, and that there is no God
to wipe away all tears from all eyes, I could go mad![21]

"Here," writes Newman, "is an argument for immortality." By
the standards of syllogistic reasoning, it is not a compelling argument, yet it may legitimately be included among the cumulation
of probabilities and experiential hints on the basis of which
human judgment is entitled to give assent to a religious proposition. As Newman puts it in one of his memorable Oxford University sermons, "A mutilated and defective evidence suffices for
persuasion where the heart is alive."[22]

This is to approach the question from the human side, from the
side of reason and experience. For Christians, however, the
approach to hope for life after death from the side of reason and
experience is a tentative one, even a troubled one. It is like the
homeward journey of the prodigal son. What is decisive here is not
the hesitant steps he takes toward his father's house, but the unre-
served welcome with which the father rushes forth to greet him.

It is often said that Christian hope for life beyond death is not
founded upon natural evidence for immortality. It is not a matter
of arriving at a philosophic faith in immortality by reasoned
steps, and then complicating this faith by adding to it the rather
more extravagant claim that there will be a resurrection, to boot.
Christian faith in life beyond death is revealed by faith in the resurrection and flows from it.

This much has been clearly established by some of the leading Protestant thinkers of our century.[23] It is an unfortunate exaggeration, however, to conclude from this that it is improper for Christians to maintain that by the natural light of reason and experience one may find grounds to hope for life beyond death.[24] There are some perfectly good reasons why Christian hope— though its categories are historical and its credentials revealed— should turn out to look, from some angles, very much like a doctrine of natural immortality.

For if God has descended into a mortal body, lived as a man, and died as a man in order to be raised up and glorified—if Christ by his death has destroyed death—then these things are true for all time. It is not an event in the past, but an event in the center of history, whose effects reach back and reach forward, embracing all who have died, all who will die, death itself.

In the *Paradiso,* Dante makes use of the rhetorical device of *hysteron proteron* to convey this idea.[25] Adam and Eve—humanity—are simultaneously fallen and redeemed, mortal and immortal, *ab origine.* They are fallen *ab origine* because their free act of disobedience has changed their nature, making them subject for all time to the rule of death. They are also redeemed *ab origine,* because the redeeming action of Christ's incarnation, passion, and resurrection has changed human nature, making it subject for all time, and beyond time, to the rule of life. These two aboriginal deeds are not on equal footing, however. Although the first aboriginal—human subjection to sin and death—is still in effect, it is the second aboriginal—the work of redemption—that is decisive, for its author is not the human will but the eternal creative

43

and salvific will of the one who calls all beings into existence. This is the mystery that, as Paul says in Ephesians 3:9, has been hidden in God through all the ages.

One may read the legend of Christ's descent into the underworld in this light, as an adventure in time travel: the heroic redeemer breaking the bonds of *kronos,* the jaws of death. What is past is no longer irrevocable once God's sacrificial love enters into the story. And God's sacrificial love enters into the story from its very beginning, as the Lamb slain from the foundation of the world.

Hence, when Christ descends into Hades it is as the Logos, calling all creation back from death. Nowhere is this expressed more vividly than in the following ancient Greek homily for Holy Saturday:

> Something strange is happening—there is a great silence on earth today, a great silence and stillness. The whole earth keeps silence because the King is asleep. The earth trembled and is still because God has fallen asleep in the flesh and he has raised up all who have slept ever since the world began. God has died in the flesh and hell trembles with fear.
>
> He has gone to search for our first parent, as for a lost sheep. Greatly desiring to visit those who live in darkness and in the shadow of death, he has gone to free from sorrow the captives Adam and Eve, he who is both God and the son of Eve. The Lord approached them bearing the cross, the weapon that had won him the victory. At the sight of him Adam, the first man he had created, struck his breast in terror and cried out to everyone: "My Lord be with you all." Christ answered him, "And with your spirit." He

took him by the hand and raised him up, saying, "Awake, O sleeper, and rise from the dead, and Christ will give you light.

"I am your God, who for your sake have become your son. Out of love for you and for your descendants I now by my own authority command all who are held in bondage to come forth, all who are in darkness to be enlightened, all who are sleeping to arise.

"I order you, O sleeper, to awake. I did not create you to be held a prisoner in hell. Rise from the dead, for I am the life of the dead. Rise up, work of my hands, you who were created in my image. Rise, let us leave this place, for you are in me and I am in you; together we form only one person and we cannot be separated."[26]

The difference between a doctrine of natural immortality and the Christian way of speaking of immortality is that Christian immortality is not an abstract quality, not something a soul possesses by rights, but an eschatological transformation that happens to a whole person—an alchemical change reaching down to one's very basest matter and transforming it into gold, into light. It happens to a whole person because it is conferred by a whole person: the person of Christ.

There is both a time-bound and a timeless aspect to this transformation—it is a mystery present eternally to the triune will of God, present temporally as the kingdom already active in our midst, present in the Eucharist as the "medicine of immortality," and present in the person of the Holy Spirit, who from the time of Christ's rising from death to glory has been poured out into the world. Nonetheless, this eschatological transformation is said to be still unfolding through time for humankind. The alchemy is at work now, but its final distillation is reserved for the world to come.

This alchemy is the consequence of God's own sacrificial descent into our mortal condition. By this action, our mortal condition is transfigured, putting on immortality. Augustine calls this action the "wonderful exchange" by which we make it possible for God to die and God makes it possible for us to live.[27] And yet it is embedded in the logic of the exchange that we must die to ourselves, must no longer belong to ourselves.[28]

Every death, every bitter separation, every uncharted change we face is part of the price we must pay for our share in the deifying light, which confers fullness of life and clarity of vision. It is a terrible price, but God paid it first, and that is our comfort.

This does not make the universe a friendly place. It is still vast beyond comprehension. There is no security except in knowing that however far and fast we fall, there is God beneath us; we are falling into God's arms.

The Right to Imagine

If the will to believe in life beyond death can be defended, then perhaps something similar can be said for the will to imagine what that life beyond death will be like—to imagine oneself as a soul, to imagine what it could mean to say "I" in a radically different form of embodiment, to imagine a state of complete fulfillment when God will be all in all, and all will be well.[29]

Such things are, strictly speaking, inconceivable. Shall we then accept Wittgenstein's prescription: "Whereof one cannot speak, thereof one must be silent"? Must we permit ourselves only a theology of the darkness of death?

On this point, I find myself in the awkward position of disagreeing with some of the most creative theological minds of our century. My conviction is that if we do not permit ourselves to form images of personal and collective existence after death, then we have no way of testing who we are or of sounding our deepest ideals. It's not that we need to know the details of the world to come—life is short and we will get our data soon enough—but we do need to imagine. This need to imagine is not a narcissistic one but a need of reason (to use Kant's language) and of common life.

We need to imagine a faraway state of consummation, a state in which every noble impulse is expressed, fulfilled, and shot through with the radiance of divine energy. We need to imagine the ideal society, the beatific vision, the communion of saints.

As Colleen McDannell and Bernhard Lang have shown in their engaging *Heaven: A History,* the history of heaven is the history of the projection of humanly constructed ideals.[30] There are theocentric and anthropocentric heavens; heavens in which the ranks of the elect are forever fixed in contemplative adoration; heavens in which friends and family are reunited for an eternity of productive labor and domestic delight; heavens for social activists, in which their favorite causes are perpetually advanced; heavens for lovers, in which both courtship and consummation are infinitely prolonged. Against the dome of the sky, each society projects its vision of the good life and of the hierarchy of values leading thereto. Here below, we struggle to balance labor and leisure, friendship and love, community life and individual fulfillment, seriousness and joy. How could we find our bearings if we did not imagine a kingdom in which all these good things are ordered and harmonized to the highest good?

Certainly it is true that such imaginings will at present tell us more about our own assumptions and longings than they do about the heavenly society. And yet we have a right to them. The effort to starve out the will to imagine has not produced the humane fruits it was expected to bring. If anything, the contrary has been shown to be the case: totalistic efforts to create utopia on earth and to suppress pie-in-the-sky thinking have ended by creating hell on earth.

The social psychologist Robert Jay Lifton makes a convincing case for the need for symbols of immortality that provide a sense of continuity in the face of death. He finds that when individuals or societies are prevented from cultivating images of death that promise continued life or transcendence, their moral energy is soon sapped and "psychic numbing" sets in. Lifton speaks of five modes of symbolic immortality: through one's children, through religious conceptions of an afterlife, through one's creative works, through identification with the cycles of nature, and through "experiential transcendence" or ecstasy.[31]

The common achievement of symbols of immortality is to offer the individual a wider cosmos within which to dwell, nourished by a rich network of social, natural, and spiritual connections. They overcome isolation, and are therefore both reasonable and adaptive, rather than illusory and regressive.

Of course, there are tawdry, banal forms of imagination about the afterlife, just as there are tawdry, sentimental forms of imagination about romantic love, hearth, and home. Everything really good, really strong, can be spoiled in this way if we allow it. For every genuine value, there is a counterfeit version lying in wait.

The banality of conceptions of the afterlife has been vividly criticized by Paul Tillich, in his 1952 Terry Lectures at Yale (published as *The Courage to Be*), his 1959 essay on "The Eternal Now," his 1962 Ingersoll Lecture at Harvard Divinity School, and several passages of the *Systematic Theology*. In a series of lectures at King's Chapel in Boston in 1959 on the topic "Estrangement and Return," Tillich speaks with great feeling on this subject. Following Heidegger, Tillich declares that the essential human predicament is this: in order to actualize ourselves we must first estrange ourselves from an original union with being. Herein lies our "finite freedom." The price we pay for this freedom is death, and the anxiety death inspires. The danger, Tillich contends, is that this anxiety will drive us to retreat into "phony answers," chief among which is a literalistic belief in life after death.

Being temporal means being in anxiety. This is the reason why the continuation of a temporal existence after death would not conquer nonbeing at all, would not conquer anxiety at all. Only the eternal now conquers it, by conquering eternally the temporal process. This is the only eternity we have, the experience in the now in which it reveals itself. But this is something different from a repetitious continuation of moments of time endlessly. I don't hesitate to call this the exact definition of hell.

Tillich's position is unequivocal: the image Christians commonly entertain of life after death he does not hesitate to call hell.

His appreciation for symbol figures less importantly here than his sense of a prophetic task to call humanity back from idolatry. For he believes that the afterlife has degenerated from a life-giving symbol into a narcissistic projection, which must be torn down in order to find an authentic relationship with the eternal. This view—that one must choose between the dream of heaven and authentic engagement with the eternal now—has won adherents among many contemporary Protestant, Catholic, and Jewish thinkers because of its inherent nobility. Certainly no one could accuse Paul Tillich of wishful thinking. Yet such austerity with regard to fundamental wishes may prove in the end to have a debilitating effect on faith.

The impulse to demythologize conceptions of the afterlife is related to the discomfort with popular and imaginative piety that has led religious intellectuals to feel embarrassed by icons and rosary beads. If we allow this embarrassment to have its way with the eschatological imagination, however, we will be left not only without consolation when death strikes, but also symbolically impoverished in many other respects. Conceptions of death and immortality are not isolated elements in a religious/cultural system. They run through every limb of the system, in a dense dark tangle, like arteries in a living body. Conceptions of death and immortality belong, as D. Z. Phillips points out, to the total religious world picture.[32] The picture may fade, may eventually be lost altogether. One thing we can be sure of, though, is that the picture will not endure if its crucial features are cut out. It is no good pretending that we do not need those features—the hole in the canvas is too obvious to miss.

THREE

Compline

Sheltered Sleep and Eternal Wakefulness—
The Antiphony of Christian Hope

The Letter on Eschatology

In May 1979 the Sacred Congregation for the Doctrine of the Faith addressed to all the Roman Catholic bishops a "Letter on Certain Questions Concerning Eschatology," providing guidelines for theological reflection on eschatological language and imagery.[1] As one might expect, the letter is a mix of affirmations and cautions. What is affirmed, above all, is the final article of the baptismal creed: "We look for the resurrection of the dead, and the life of the world to come." The letter explains that "the Church understands this resurrection as referring to *the whole person;* for the elect it is nothing other than the extension to human beings of the Resurrection of Christ itself."

At the same time, the letter gives cautious approval to the traditional ways of speaking about the soul's continued existence

after death: "The Church affirms that a spiritual element survives and subsists after death, an element endowed with consciousness and will, so that the 'human self' subsists."[2]

The letter endorses the continued use of the word "soul" because, though inexact, it is a widely recognized way to affirm continued existence. The anthropological difficulties that arise are not sufficient reason for eliminating the word. What matters most, the letter maintains, is to keep in sight the Church's central confession of faith and to avoid "every way of thinking or speaking that would render meaningless or unintelligible her prayers, her funeral rites and the religious acts offered for the dead."

The provisional and pragmatic character of this statement is in striking contrast to the letter's very definitive way of speaking about the resurrection of the dead, the Assumption of the Virgin Mary, and the expectation of the glorious manifestation of Christ. The details of belief about the soul and the interim period between death and resurrection are deliberately left vague. The letter warns against speculative excesses, pointing out that "neither Scripture nor theology provides sufficient light for a proper picture of life after death." It is enough to know, the letter says, that

> we shall be with Christ and "we shall see God" (cf. 1 Jn. 3:2), and it is in these promises and marvellous mysteries that our hope essentially consists. Our imagination may be incapable of reaching these heights, but our heart does so instinctively and completely.

This is one case, I believe, in which the chastening of curiosity has a liberating effect—like Kant's restricting of theoretical reason to make room for faith, but with a broader religious program. The limits to speculation having been carefully drawn, it becomes possible within those limits to give fuller recognition to the workings of the eschatological imagination, its cultural history, and its diverse forms.

With that in mind, let us now consider the bearing of near-death testimony on three knotty questions of Christian eschatology: anthropological dualism, the interim period between death and resurrection, and judgment of the dead. This will bring us to some concluding reflections on the interplay of wakefulness and rest as the antiphony of Christian hope.

Dualisms Reconsidered

One often hears it said that dualism is the besetting vice of Western thought. We have inherited a life-denying, world-rejecting, dichotomous way of thinking, we are told; the language of soul-body dualism, in particular, is blamed for everything from the despoiling of the environment to the oppression of women.[3]

What this critique overlooks is the great variety of dualisms. One familiar dualism is the metaphysical doctrine that views body and soul as distinct orders of being. Occasionally this dualism has amounted to an outright declaration of war, as in the saying of the ascetic, "It kills me, so I kill it." The idea that the body is the enemy, the prison, or the tomb of the soul can be found in literature of Platonic origin, but only as one among many ways of articulating the mysteries of selfhood and the challenge of the philosophic quest. The body is also, in the Platonic tradition, the indispensable means by which we are to engage in our essential calling as seekers of truth and lovers of the good. In ascetic traditions, the language of metaphysical dualism is employed to marshal forces for the contest with temptation, for self-overcoming, for sacrificial self-giving. Christian asceticism dies to the world— that is, to its death-dealing powers and principalities, obsessions, and addictions. Except in its extreme forms, however, Christian asceticism, even when it uses the language of metaphysical dualism, is not a death wish for the body or for the natural world.

Only one kind of metaphysical dualism belongs essentially to Christianity, and that is the dualism of life against death, as we hear in the Easter sequence "Victimae paschali laudes": death and life confront each other in a prodigious battle; the prince of life takes death upon himself, ransoms death's captives, and brings them into his kingdom.[4]

The following hymn by Prudentius for the burial of the dead is strongly dualistic in its anthropological imagery, yet the overriding theme is not the independent sovereignty of the soul over the body, so much as the ultimate sovereignty of the Creator over the whole person and the final victory of life over death. In this life, flesh wars against spirit (as in his allegorical epic poem the *Psychomachia*). Yet God, who created body and soul together, intends to reunite them, and Prudentius does not hesitate to remind God of this promise.

> God, the blazing fountain of our souls,
> who joined two elements, one living
> and the other dying, to create
> man out of your divine fatherhood,

remember that both are yours. For you
they were combined, it is you they serve
while together they cling, flesh and soul,
stirred and moved by the life you give them.

When they separate man is finished:
the thirsty earth welcomes the body
and a breath of air takes the spirit;
each part of man goes back to its source.

All created things in time weaken
and waste away: things joined together
must be separated; things composed
of contrary parts must come undone.

But you, O God, have shown us that death
can be conquered; you show us a way
by which those men who have died will rise
again. So long as nobility

is cut down by our mortality
as though it were locked in a prison,
that part which comes to us from Heaven
will always prove itself the stronger.

If, by chance, a worldly longing wants
to taste the mud and enjoy the earth,
the spirit too will be deflected
and follow the body's direction.

But if the fire remembers its source
and rejects the stifling contagion,
it will take with it all of the flesh;
body and soul will live in the stars.[5]

Underlying this hymn is a world picture that, as Peter Brown has shown, pervaded the Western Mediterranean world of late antiquity. According to this world picture, the body belongs to the sublunary realm of change and corruption, and the soul belongs to the superlunary realm of eternity and light. At death each part returns to its source. During the period between death and resurrection, Prudentius envisages the body as sleeping in the grave (and receiving the tender ministrations of the living) while the soul waits, resting yet wakeful, for the time of blessed reunion.

The dualism is undeniable, the idiom frankly unbiblical; nonetheless it is subsumed into a thoroughly Christian metaphysic of creation and resurrection, of life overcoming death. Consequently, it is a dualism converted—reborn, one might even say— into holism. The key statement is "remember that both are yours."

Many of our misreadings of such dramatic texts come from viewing them anachronistically through the lens of a popularized and exaggerated Cartesian dualism: the body as machine, the mind as ghost in the machine. In this kind of dualism, human nature is parsed into two utterly different kinds of thing: the *res cogitans* and the *res extensa* (the thing that thinks and the thing that occupies space), and we are left with no satisfactory way of accounting for the relationship between them. Since it has proved impossible to give an adequate account of consciousness or of personal identity by means of this language of substance, many contemporary theologians and philosophers have concluded that body-soul dualism is bankrupt.

The history of modern philosophy is to a great extent the history of attempts to overcome the dualistic model of body and mind while saving its more attractive features. Perhaps one day a more adequate solution will be found; but it is unrealistic to expect religious anthropologies to conform to what is at best a fragile consensus among contemporary scientists, social critics, and philosophers, or to what is really only a recent reconstruction of the biblical norm. The more enduring criteria by which to judge anthropological models are their fruits for religious life and their capacity to call to mind what is centrally important in the Christian confession.

In any case, the anthropological dualisms that are proper to the Christian tradition are for the most part, as Bultmann long ago pointed out, not metaphysical but moral, representing not two substances but two existential options: one may choose to walk according to the flesh or according to the spirit. In that case, the word "soul" represents the deepest level at which one makes such a choice; it is the "I" that makes moral commitments or drifts toward moral chaos.[6] In Christian anthropologies the soul has a dynamic character; it gravitates, by the power of love; it moves up and down the scale of being; it is never merely a static substance to which the accidents of personality are unrelated.

In Defense of Soul Talk

When my son John was five, he persuaded me of the continuing relevance of soul talk. We had just enjoyed a very long walk, during which he collected signs of spring and kept a running tally of bits of litter. As we drew near our house, he reminded me that I had promised to help him build a robot. I explained that I was much too tired to make a robot. John remonstrated, "But Mommy, don't you know, you are not your body!" "What am I, then?" I asked. "You are your soul—and your soul is as big as the universe," came the authoritative reply. Thinking to stump him, I said, "Well then, why am I so tired?" John thought for a few seconds and said, "It must be chemicals." I had no wish to scold him for his ontological dualism; at the moment, it seemed to serve.

Similarly, the study of near-death testimony has convinced me that Christian eschatology must inevitably resort to some form of soul-body dualism. If soul language has gone into eclipse, then I believe it is due to return, for reasons that I shall now indicate.

In common usage, the word "soul" functions rhetorically as a synecdoche, a part that stands for the whole. But it stands for the whole in a special way. Since it is not the term by which people are usually identified, it has a special aura. Even though I should like my friends to meet soul to soul, it would be poor etiquette for me to introduce them by saying, "Soul of Catherine, allow me to present the soul of James."

The word "soul" is reserved for special occasions, such as liturgy, poetry, and private prayer, when one wishes to say "I" not just in the ordinary way but in the deepest possible way: "Praise the Lord, O my soul, and all that is within me, praise his holy name." On such occasions "soul" refers to the whole self, to all that is within me; and it seems to me that it does a better job of representing my whole self than that thin, wobbly pronoun "I," which is liable to being taken hostage by whatever obsession is temporarily in command.

The pronoun "I" is often little more than a counter set down on the roulette table, to stand in for the interests of the ego-self while the wheel spins. "Soul," on the other hand, translates *anima,* with reminiscences of *spiritus* and *animus.* Compared to our abstract ways of speaking about the human person, it conveys a much richer cluster of imaginative associations: the breath that animates my frame, the values that animate my life, the mind and spirit that animate the world.

I use the word "soul" properly to refer not to some hidden organ or inviolate substance within me but to my whole self, gathered together. This is what Antony Flew failed to recognize when he made his famous remark that "the news of the immortality of my soul would be of no more concern to me than the news that my appendix would be preserved eternally in a bottle."[7]

The word "soul" has connotations that are at once sacrificial, eschatological, and ecstatic. The soul is the harvest of the self, gathered up and brought before the altar. It is the self at the moment of death and on the day of judgment. I find my soul when I am in *ex-stasis,* beside myself, by virtue of an intimate relationship with another, divine or human. Even when Christian writers imagine the soul as an inner chamber, it is never perfectly enclosed upon itself; it is a bridal chamber, a place of expectancy. It could never be a purely private realm, for someone else holds the key.

The word "flesh" also does a good job of representing the

whole person, particularly when the context is one of collective destiny or public witnessing of communal events: "all flesh shall see it together." The eschatological meaning here is unmistakable, and the dualism helps rather than hinders its dramatic impact; to convert the phrase to "all people shall see it together" is to make it insipid. The dynamic character of the words "soul" and "flesh" is due precisely to their incompleteness and polarity; together they hint at the mystery of a self that exceeds the sum of its parts and remains incomplete until the last day.

How unfortunate, then, that the *anima* and its vernacular companions have begun to disappear from liturgical texts. "Lord I am not worthy that you should come under my roof. Speak but the word and my soul shall be healed" has given way to the more abstract petition "Lord I am not worthy to receive you. Only say the word and I shall be healed." The background to this petition—the centurion's appeal for the bodily healing of his servant (Matthew 8:8)—is thereby effaced, so that the effect is, inadvertently, a spiritualizing one. No gain in wholeness, but a loss of personal concreteness results from suppression of soul talk.

Similarly, Joseph Cardinal Ratzinger has argued that the ultimate effect of suppressing soul language has been, strangely, to spiritualize the idea of the resurrection.[8] According to Ratzinger, what began as a campaign against dualism turned into a new and more intractable form of dualism. Having given up speaking of souls abiding in an interim state, one is almost compelled to speak of resurrection taking place within the very experience of death.[9]

The advantage of this resurrection-in-death model is that it preserves the reality of death, honors the absolute transcendence of eternity, and communicates the profound Christian value of self-abandonment. Its chief disadvantage, as Ratzinger points out, is that it reduces the resurrection to a metaphorical way of speaking about being in Christ. At the same time, it diminishes the stock of images upon which we need to draw if we are to visualize the participation in eternal life of the whole person (including the human body) and the historical experience of humankind. The story of life, according to this model, ends with each person's death. For it was the soul that until recently served as placeholder, keeping the story of life open until the consummation of historical time.

The systematic removal of soul talk from the rites for death and burial has had a similarly distancing effect. Despite its troubled philosophical history, the word "soul" has been a sturdy vehicle for conveying the sense of vital connection between the society of the living and the society of the dead. Since it seems unlikely that a good substitute will be found in the near future, the Letter on Eschatology justly warns against dispensing with it.

What we learn from our study of near-death testimony amplifies this point by demonstrating that dualistic language has an important imaginative function. The out-of-body experience is the visionary concretizing of what is nearly a universal idea: that death is the giving up or sending forth of one's spirit, soul, or vital breath. Not only death, but deep sleep, has been understood by most cultures, imagistically, as the sending forth of one's spirit.

The people who testify to near-death experience are neither

Platonists nor Cartesians, yet they find it natural to speak of leaving their bodies in this way. There simply is no other way for the imagination to dramatize the experience of death: the soul quits the body and yet continues to have a form.

The form of the soul is another cause for embarrassment: in visionary reports, as in artistic depictions (which must obey similar laws of visual representation), the soul appears in quasi-corporeal guise, as a ball of light, a bit of luminous fog, a crystalline sphere, or a *homunculus*—a naked, childlike replica of the body, which departs the body through the mouth or the crown of the head.[10]

To attempt to shore up such descriptions with esoteric physiologies is to evade the basic point: such physiologies come and go, but dualism and somatomorphism are inescapable laws governing the imaginative construction of the sense of self. Moreover, to eliminate dualistic and somatomorphic language is to cut ourselves off from centuries of tradition, both doctrinal and aesthetic. It would be a great loss if we became incapable of reading John Donne without making mental reservations.

What our study of near-death testimony shows, in short, is the folly of trying to suppress imagistic ways of thinking about death. If new images are needed, let them emerge from our own experience and reflection, or even from playful experiment. The notion that certain symbols should be eliminated because they are obsolete is a misguided premise of contemporary theological reflection and an unnecessary cause of symbolic impoverishment. We should bear in mind that the archaism of symbols is part of their appeal, that some symbols may go into retirement only to return in full vigor at a future time, and that religious traditions are better served by a plurality of symbols than by forced consistency.

The Interim State

Similar considerations apply to the problem of the interim state. What happens between the moment of death and the day of resurrection? This has been a puzzling question not just for Christianity but for all traditions that envision a collective end time: Jewish, Islamic, Zoroastrian, even Buddhist.

In Christianity, the interim period did not receive the kind of dogmatic definition that was given to the resurrection of the dead for it was not so intimately tied to the original *kerygma* or to the development of Christological and Trinitarian doctrine. The early indeterminacy of Christian views of the interim period left the field open for a variety of visualizations, drawing upon biblical and postbiblical Jewish imagery that envisioned the dead variously as gathered to the fathers, enjoying refreshment in the paradise of the martyrs, resting in the bosom of Abraham, waiting under the altar of the heavenly Temple, or waiting under the throne of God. These Jewish images were recast, however, in relationship to Christ, following the cue in Luke 23:43, where Jesus says to the good thief, "Today you will be with me in paradise."

From now on, Luke suggests, all who die in Christ will be with Christ. Even if the interim period is envisaged according to the archaic imagery of Sheol, it is no longer Sheol as a house of dust cut off from the remembrance of God, but Sheol as a place of refreshment, upon which has already descended the "dew of light" of which Isaiah 26:19 speaks.

The Protestant tradition has tended, beginning with Luther, to reduce the repertoire of images for the interim period to the single image of sleep, in order to discourage a belief in an active, conscious interim period (or, in other words, purgatory). Yet what is remarkable is that the Christian tradition as a whole has been willing to permit a crowd of diverse images to coexist: Sheol and paradise, sleep and refreshment. Moreover, the dead are also imagined as existing, simultaneously, in their graves. This image is necessitated not so much by theological reflection as by the universal practice of care for one's dead kin at their burial sites, and of pilgrimage to the saints, who are experienced as really present in their relics and tombs.

A study of the anthropology of funeral practices makes it immediately obvious why one should not overorganize conceptions of the interim period. For every culture whose death ways have been carefully documented by anthropologists, the evidence has emerged that communal memory assigns to the dead more than one place of continued existence, more than one moment of death, more than one instance of postmortem reckoning, and more than one way of picturing and naming personal identity.[11] In some societies, this plurality finds expression in the practice of multiple burials. As in the Alfred Hitchcock film *The Trouble with Harry,* the dead are buried, exhumed, and reburied as many times as it takes to mark the series of intermediate moments of death.[12] The purpose is to lead both the dead and the mourners safely through the various stations of a long and perilous journey;

by the end of this journey, if all goes well, the dead person will have become fully assimilated to the ancestors.

Proliferation and redundancy of images for postmortem existence is therefore the norm; the effort to cook them down to a single conception has never been shown to succeed. Indeed, if it were to succeed, it would render unintelligible many of the things people do for the dead. Again, this would mean the breaking of vital links between the society of the living and the dead— the outcome would be not clarity, but anomie and despair.

An Imaginal World?

So far, I have suggested that in near-death experience, the visionary steps through the gate of an imaginative encounter with death into an imaginal world. I do not want to give the impression, however, that I am proposing a theory of the afterlife state as an imaginal or dreamlike realm. Such a theory could be constructed by drawing, for instance, on Tibetan Buddhist conceptions of the *bar-do* (the intermediate state between rebirths), Australian myths of the dream time, Jungian interpretations of the psyche's descent into the underworld, or one of the newer holographic or cybernetic models of consciousness.

It is especially tempting to develop a theory of this kind to deal with the interim period. When treated as an intramental or intrapsychic state, the interim period is rendered less philosophically problematic; and it also becomes easier to reconcile Christian eschatology with the dizzying variety of eschatological scenarios from other traditions.

I have deliberately avoided constructing a theory of the other world along such speculative lines, however. Efforts to use current scientific vocabulary to naturalize the other world inevitably date very quickly, as the history of the spiritualist movement—with its quaint theories about ether and electromagnetism—attests. Moreover, what may be intriguing as a thought-experiment can become, if converted into theory, an unwarranted speculative intrusion into a realm that is properly mysterious (*vana curiositas!*). The proper function of our conceptions of the afterlife is to provide not knowledge but orientation.

The other world is imaginative on this side, the only side we know. But we will not have framed a satisfying picture of the afterlife if we think of it as merely dreamlike, or as one among many possible worlds projected by human consciousness and culture. People who report near-death experiences insist that their state of awareness was not dreamlike but startlingly lucid—if anything, more real than life seems here below. It is as if they were given, within a dream, an intimation of what it would be like to be fully awake. And this intimation accords with a fundamental feature of Christian eschatological hope. What Christians hope for is not a pleasant dream but a complete awakening, compared to which our present existence will look like troubled sleep. What Christians hope for, finally, is a collective awakening, an entry into a real world, compared to which our present world is almost fallen into non-being. And in that real world, Christians hope, every memory worth saving will be saved, every value eternally upheld, every species and person preserved.

A saying that Plutarch attributes to Heraclitus suggests the same idea: "Among those who sleep, each one is withdrawn into a world of his own; only those who are awake have a world in common."[13] It is for nothing less than this common world that Christians hope; but the Christian tradition has also had the realism to know that it will not be ushered in by individual effort, political action, scientific progress, or programs for planetary consciousness raising; nor will it arrive at any historical moment short of the eschaton. Even so, the common world of which eschatology dreams impinges on this fragmented world and gives it hope.

The Judgment of the Dead

Christians may also dare to hope, as Hans Urs von Balthasar has argued, for the eventual salvation of all humankind.[14] For the hope that all may be saved is not the same as the optimistic assertion of an *apokatastasis pantōn* (universal restoration) that cancels human freedom by denying all possibility of loss.[15]

What shall we say, then, of the proliferation of imaginative scenarios for the judgment of the dead and the eternal condemnation of the wicked? As Balthasar suggests, the problem with these scenarios has been their deployment by a theological tradition that tried to know too much, and took pleasure from the torment of the unjust.

One could also include, under the heading of the problem of knowing too much, the extreme forms of millennialist eschatological expectation that are a feature of some contemporary fundamentalist, Marian, and New Age movements.

If, on the other hand, we admit our ignorance and acknowledge the imaginative character of judgment scenarios, we gain the opportunity for what Paul Ricoeur has called a second naïveté. What would a second naïveté look like with regard to postmortem judgment? Again, we are dealing with a theologically troublesome idea that is nonetheless an inescapable feature of religious eschatologies. And on this subject too, the study of near-death reports has some surprising lessons for us.

I have mentioned that one of the striking features of contemporary near-death literature is the absence of hell, purgatory, and postmortem punishment. This is partly attributable to the liberal proclivities of the researchers; markedly different results are reported by conservative evangelical Christians who have studied near-death phenomena. But if notions of sin and punishment are suppressed in the popular accounts, there is, nonetheless, plenty of evidence for the persistence—though in camouflaged form—of the notion of judgment. The form in which the motif of judgment persists is the "life review."

The Life Review

Although not an inevitable feature of near-death reports, the life-review episode occurs in a wide variety of narratives.[16] Even before the term "near-death experience" was coined, the idea that a drowning man sees his life pass before him had been planted in the popular imagination (where it quickly acquired the status of proverbial wisdom) by its treatment in several widely read nineteenth-century English and American memoirs and medical essays. A famous example is the anecdote from De Quincey's *Confessions of an English Opium-Eater:*

> I was once told by a near relative of mine that, having in her childhood fallen into a river, and being on the very verge of death but for the assistance which reached her at the last critical moment, she saw in a moment her whole life, clothed in its forgotten incidents, arrayed before her as in a mirror, not successively, but simultaneously; and she had a faculty developed as suddenly for comprehending the whole and every part.[17]

In his book *Euthanasia or Medical Treatment in the Aid of Easy Dying* (1887), Dr. William Munk, a prominent medical essayist, relates the experience of the famous British naval officer Admiral Beaufort when he fell off a ship into Portsmouth harbor as a young boy. As soon as Beaufort stopped struggling, a feeling of contentment swept over him; his mind became calm but at the same time alert and invigorated, and he found himself reviewing his life in reverse chronological order:

> the whole period of my existence seemed to be placed before me in a kind of panoramic review, and each act of it seemed to be accompanied by a consciousness of right or wrong, or by some reflection on its cause or its consequences; indeed, many trifling events which had been long forgotten, then crowded into my imagination, and with the character of recent familiarity.[18]

In 1892 the Swiss geologist and alpinist Albert Heim published an article on thirty mountain climbers, himself among them, who had survived nearly fatal falls. Most of the survivors Heim interviewed reported having felt calm, lucid, even joyful as they rushed headlong toward death. Many spoke of a life review. Heim's own account is typical:

> I saw my whole past life take place in many images, as though on a stage at some distance from me. I saw myself as the chief character in the performance. Everything was transfigured as though by a heavenly light and everything was beautiful without grief, without anxiety, and without pain.
>
> . . . I acted out my life, as though I were an actor on a stage upon which I looked down from practically the highest gallery in the theatre. Both hero and onlooker, I was as though doubled.[19]

Among the common features are the sense of the self as a spectator, the attitude of serene detachment, the comprehensiveness and simultaneity of the visual replay of memories, and the implication that the life review constitutes a final summation and judgment of one's character and history.

A striking parallel to the life review can be found in the phenomenon of "elderly reminiscence," in which childhood memories flood the mind as if to compensate for the failing of memory associated with old age, and which many psychologists interpret as a way of achieving integration before death.[20] For those who face death suddenly or prematurely and are thus deprived of this experience of gradually collecting and reviewing images of the past, the life review perhaps serves as an accelerated way to accomplish one of life's essential tasks. Similarly, psychologists have noticed parallels between the life review and the vivid visual replay of memories that sometimes accompanies bereavement.[21]

If death sets the seal on one's identity, then the life review is the narrative act by which one becomes a whole person, a person whose life story is complete.[22] The panoramic and instantaneous character of this review is particularly significant, for it suggests that one is no longer, as Augustine lamented, torn between time past and time to come. All times have been gathered together, all past experiences witnessed and offered up in a comprehensive and simultaneous thought that distantly mirrors the comprehensive and simultaneous wholeness of divine thought. This is precisely the kind of memory to which Augustine appealed when he set out to make his *confessio*, or sacrificial offering of his life story to God and to the reader.

So far, I have suggested that the life review is a completing of the life story and a gathering together of one's memories to make of oneself a whole offering, a perfect holocaust, at the moment of the imagined encounter with death. In what sense, though, is the life review analogous to postmortem judgment? It corresponds to one of the most common symbolic modalities for postmortem judgment: the encounter with one's deeds in externalized form, for example, recorded in a book, weighed upon a scale, reflected in a mirror, or dramatized, as in a psychomachy, by a pitched battle of virtues against vices.

The third-century apocalypse known to the West as the *Visio Pauli* depicts the soul's exit from the body as a critical moment in which the entire history of one's actions and intentions is displayed in visible form: first, as a written record of deeds and then as a confrontation with the souls whom one has injured in life. In one medieval version of this text an angel asks Paul, "Have you believed and known, that whatever each one of you has done, he sees in the hour of his need?" The scriptural basis for this comes from 1 Corinthians 3, where Paul says that "every man's work shall be made manifest" on the day of the Lord, and shall be tested by fire. What is striking in this medieval version of the apocalypse of Paul is that the encounter with deeds has been transferred from the day of the Lord to the time of death.

Similarly, in the *Dialogues* of Gregory the Great, those who die and return report seeing their good and evil works made manifest in the form of symbolic buildings, personifications, and dramatic encounters. Gregory interprets the other world entirely as a symbolic landscape, in which the visionary confronts his own soul and thus brings judgment upon himself.

Two developments in the medieval Christian motif of encounter with deeds are especially worthy of note:

1. The transfer of judgment from the Last Day to the interim period and from the interim period to the deathbed. Judgment thereby becomes an expected part of the near-death experience, as well as an anticipated scenario for end times. The redundancy was apparently not considered a problem.

2. A change in the character of this encounter, from an impartial modality of judgment to a contest between mercy and judgment. In several medieval return-from-death accounts, visionaries read the record of their sins only to discover that a few tears, looked upon kindly by the Blessed Virgin or the Lord, will be enough to erase the record. In the fifteenth-century illustrated

artes moriendi (guidebooks on the art, or craft, of dying), the record of deeds (looking for all the world like one of those old-fashioned computer punch cards that must not be bent, spindled, or mutilated) is in the hands of the demons, who wave it in the dying man's face in order to tempt him to despair. The angels make use of the same record only when they need to provide countervailing force against the temptation to vainglory or over-confidence. More often than not, the role of the angelic party is to try to destroy the damaging evidence. Thus the encounter with deeds becomes an object lesson in the need to take refuge in divine mercy and, above all, in the intercession of the Blessed Virgin and the saints.

If we turn to the vestiges of this motif as they occur in con-temporary near-death testimony, these two points have striking relevance, even if we accept the view that our culture is post-Christian. First, the transfer of judgment to the deathbed stuck; the emphasis is on the individual as he or she meets death. This emphasis on the individual heightens anxiety and therefore increases the need for consoling reassurances. Second, the encounter with deeds is, for the reason I just mentioned, an occa-sion to be reassured about one's worth. The only reason the appeal for mercy is not heard so clearly today is that the encounter with deeds is from start to finish a reassuring and therapeutic exercise. There is no sense of being judged by an external being; rather, the emphasis is on self-evaluation, learn-ing, and growth.

The following example is typical:

And into this great peace that I had become there came the life of Phyllis parading past my view. . . . The reliving included not only the deeds committed by Phyllis since her birth in 1937 in Twin Falls, Idaho, but also a reliving of every thought ever thought and every word ever spoken PLUS the effect of every thought, word and deed upon everyone and anyone who had ever come within her sphere of influence whether she actually knew them or not PLUS the effect of her every thought, word and deed upon the weather, the soil, plants and animals, the water, everything else. . . . I never before realized that we were responsible and accountable for EVERY SINGLE THING WE DID. That was overwhelming!

It was me judging me, not some heavenly St. Peter. And my judgment was critical and stern. I was not satisfied with many, many things Phyllis had done, said or thought. There was a feeling of sadness and failure, yet a growing feeling of joy when the realization came that Phyllis had always done SOMETHING. . . . She tried. Much of what she did was constructive and positive. She learned and grew in her learning. This was satisfying. Phyllis was okay.[23]

This much we can say for the judgment scenarios of contemporary near-death testimony: although they may be excessively privatistic and optimistic, they at least avoid the unbecoming trait of taking satisfaction in contemplating the doom of others. If we step back and take the long view of the history of judgment motifs in Christian eschatology, we can see that modulated by the many—even redundant—media of forgiveness and reconciliation, the anticipation of judgment is part of what gives life meaning and direction. It completes the life story and thus provides the necessary prelude to the consummation of our common life.

When we speak of that consummation, we move entirely beyond the range of near-death testimony. Nonetheless, the study of near-death experience has alerted us to features of the eschatological imagination that remain in play even here. It has taught us the need for a plurality of images to convey what is, from a mortal vantage point, a scarcely conceivable hope. When it comes to portraying the final consummation of that hope, images fail. Yet before they fail, they lead us to the threshold.

Eternal Wakefulness and Eternal Rest: The Antiphony of Christian Hope

John Donne has written "One short sleepe past, we wake eternally." Actually, though, Christian hope is for both at once: eternal wakefulness and peaceful sleep. Neither image by itself will do. Sleep by itself begins to sound like extinction; waking by itself begins to sound like a restless insomnia or an unbroken tedium. With enough coffee in me, I can imagine what it would be like to stay awake forever, but not without an underlying feeling of desperate longing for sleep. What we really want is both the refreshment of sleep and the rapture of waking. This is the antiphony of Christian hope, and it is beautifully expressed by the hymns and antiphons for Compline, the lullaby with which the Church sings itself to sleep.

These themes can be found compressed in the little antiphon "Salva Nos," which frames the Nunc Dimittis (when Simeon says he is ready to die, now that he has held the Holy Child) in the Night Office:

> Salva nos Domine vigilantes,
> Custodi nos dormientes,
> Ut vigilemus cum Christo,
> et requiescamus in pace.

> O Lord keep us safe throughout our waking hours,
> Protect us while we sleep,
> That we may watch with Christ,
> and rest with him in peace.[24]

To watch with Christ is to recapture the mood of vigilant expectancy with which the first Christians awaited the *parousia,* both as a future event and as a mysterious manifestation in the present. The Eucharist is celebrated in the same eschatological mood, combining wakefulness before the divine presence with remembrance of a past event and longing for its fulfillment in glory. In the Divine Office, however, the eschatological mood is brought into everyday consciousness, as one entrusts oneself to divine protection in the rhythms of night and day, waking and sleeping. Perhaps this day will not be the critical one on which the battle between death and life is decisively waged; yet we know that today countless human beings will be born and will die, while those of us who receive our births or deaths on other days live out the same theme transposed to a minor key, laboring in the day and resting at night. Waking and resting are natural symbols that, by their association with the paschal mystery, become eschatological signs.

In itself, eternal wakefulness is inconceivable, the prospect unbearable. Many legends convey this idea. When Gilgamesh fails to stay awake in the house of the flood hero for the seven nights required of him, he proves that human beings are not fit for eternal life. In the Gospel, at the critical moments of disclosure, of Christ's glory on Mt. Tabor and of his agony at Gethsemani, the disciples are similarly overcome by sleep. What these narratives suggest is that by their unaided powers human beings cannot sustain vigilance. It can come only as a gift, and before the gift can be received, the recipient must be remade.

Along with eternal wakefulness, Christian eschatology holds out the promise of eternal rest and unalloyed security. It is this sense of security for which the Office of Compline prays: "May the Lord Almighty grant us a quiet night and a perfect end." The opening hymns for Compline alternate between songs of praise for the radiant divine light that confers eternal wakefulness (such as the *Phos hilaron*) and songs of petition for the protective shade that confers safety from insomnia and bad dreams.

What is sought is not a blinkered security, but the kind of security that comes from entrusting oneself unreservedly to the truth, who is the one being entirely worthy of trust. The responsory sung at Compline, "Into thy hands, O Lord, I commend my spirit," conveys a feeling of being protected, even though the words call to mind the prospect of death and the *commendatio animae* that marks the moment of death. Why do they convey such a sense of security? Why should it be comforting to be reminded of death just before sleep?

The comforting effect is due in part to the way these words

ritualize the experience of sleep and death, overcoming the individual's isolation just at the moment when he or she is about to slip into darkness. The *commendatio animae* is not a private prayer but a communal send-off, spoken on behalf of the dying by the society of the living. And when it pronounces the moment of death, it also announces the assimilation of the Christian soul into the society of the blessed dead. It is a "performative utterance" that ushers the soul from one company to another, safely escorting it through the liminal state of isolation and death. It is like tossing a rope bridge across the chasm of nonbeing that separates the two worlds.

Most important, because the words "Into thy hands, O Lord, I commend my spirit" come first from the Psalter and then from the Cross, they are words of hope rather than of resignation. What might otherwise be a blind gamble or a stoic acquiescence to the ordinances of the world soul becomes an act of taking refuge. It is the precise equivalent of the child's prayer: "Now I lay me down to sleep, I pray the Lord my soul to keep. If I should die before I wake, I pray the Lord my soul to take."[25]

The prayers of Compline seek protection not only from the great terrors recounted in Psalm 91—the snare of the fowler, the plague that prowls in the darkness—but also from the little disturbances that trouble sleep, the *noctium phantasmata*:

> Te lucis ante terminum
> Rerum Creator poscimus
> Ut solita clementia
> Sis praesul ad custodiam.

Procul recedant somnia,
Et noctium phantasmata:
Hostempue nostrum comprime,
Ne polluantur corpora.

O Father, Maker of all things,
We pray to you at evening light:
With your unfailing clemency,
Bring us in safety through the night.

From phantom-shapes that haunt our sleep,
And evil dreams, make us secure.
Defeat our ancient enemy,
And from defilement keep us pure.[26]

The last song sung before sleep is sung to Mary, the mother of mercy, whose welcome ends the banishment of the sons and daughters of Eve. The Salve Regina is the fulfillment of the *commendatio animae,* the perfect end, when the pilgrim is embraced at long last by his loving advocate and all fear of doom dissolves.

When I have to tuck my son into his covers for the twelfth time, check under the bed for slimy monsters, and reassure him about the latest metaphysical puzzle he is pondering, it can make me quite impatient. But when the moment finally arrives for him to sink into his pillow with the sigh that tells me he feels completely secure and surrounded by love, I cannot help seeing this as a preview of heaven, partial though it may be.

Clearly, an adequate picture of eternal life (I did not say accurate, just adequate for the purposes of religious life) requires us to draw upon images and to combine qualities that in our present condition are incompatible. The future life must be imagined as a time of wakefulness and rest, light and shadow, judgment and mercy, security and adventure. Whatever else it may be, the future life cannot be boring; all arguments from the premise that it would be boring are simply failures of imagination.

At the close of the *City of God,* Augustine gives us his preview: "On that day we shall rest and see, see and love, love and praise."[27] The pivot of the sentence is love. With an imagination schooled by love, Augustine is able to envision the day when such apparent incompatibles will coexist: the peace of eternal rest, the intellectual fulfillment of contemplative vision, and the ceaseless industry of communal praise.

Banality in our conceptions of the afterlife results from fastening onto one set of images to the exclusion of others. Profound conceptions of the afterlife are characterized by the *coincidentia oppositorum* of which Cusanus and Carl Jung and Rudolf Otto have spoken. Along with reassurance, they convey a sense of an unfathomable mystery, *tremendum et fascinans.*

I conclude with these thoughts. We have seen indications of the persistence of the eschatological imagination—enough, I hope, to persuade us that Christian eschatology is reducible neither to politics nor to a general attitude of hopefulness, and that it is not a distraction from life but a way of orienting oneself to life. Christian eschatology is the story of divine love calling creation back from death, a story that can be told only by drawing upon a repertoire of images that is endlessly varied and at times seemingly at variance with itself: sleep, waking, marriage, feasting, homecoming. All of these images are needed. None of them is sufficient or exact. Ultimately we must say, with Dante, "Here power fails the high phantasy" and let love lead us the rest of the way.

Notes

One

1. *The New Yorker* (January 24, 1988), p. 46.

2. F. X. Durrwell, *The Resurrection: A Biblical Study* (London: Sheed and Ward, 1960), p. 38. Thanks to Sr. Mary Paula Wenzel, O.S.B., for bringing this to my attention.

3. 1 Cor. 15:22, 2 Cor. 5:17, Rom. 8:2, Eph. 2:6. See Durrwell, *The Resurrection*, pp. 28ff.

4. Raymond J. DeMallie, ed., *The Sixth Grandfather: Black Elk's Teachings Given to John G. Neihardt* (Lincoln and London: University of Nebraska Press, 1984), p. 226. This statement comes directly from the transcript of the interviews with Neihardt. In *Black Elk Speaks* (Lincoln: University of Nebraska Press, 1961), first published in 1932, Neihardt gives the following rendition: "From that time on, I always got up very early to see the rising of the daybreak star. People knew that I did this, and many would get up to see it with me, and when it came we said: 'Behold the star of understanding!'" p. 176.

5. In a later series of interviews granted to Neihardt in 1944, Black Elk noted that this practice was also associated with the rites of burial. For four days after a burial, the relatives would try to see the morning star every morning. Black Elk commented on the moral significance of this practice: "The Indians believed a man could change his mode of living at this time; he could form a better habit of life than he had before. That is a good time to change to become a better man. If you get up to see the morning star for four days and do your work early and be nice to people, you will form good habits." DeMallie, *The Sixth Grandfather,* p. 382.

6. Morning hymn, Clement of Alexandria, *Protrepticus* 9, 84:2; cf. Eph. 5:14, Isa. 60:1.

7. Introduction to Leo Tolstoy, *The Death of Ivan Ilyich,* tr. Lyn Solotaroff (Toronto and New York: Bantam Books, 1981), p. 20.

8. *The New York Times* (March 8, 1989).

9. *New Age Journal* (April 1986).

10. Notable here is the theme of energy, a contemporary idiom for spirit. The whole piece is an expression of "energy-materialism," in which the soul is not distinguished from matter but is matter rarefied.

11. George Santayana, *The Life of Reason,* 2nd ed. (New York: Charles Scribner's Sons, 1942–51), vol. 3, p. 237.

12. Sigmund Freud, "Thoughts for the Times on War and Death" (1915) in *Collected Papers,* authorized translation under the supervision of Joan Rivière (London and New York, 1959), vol. 4, pp. 304–5.

13. John Bowker, *The Meanings of Death* (Cambridge: Cambridge University Press, 1991).

14. Oscar Cullman, "Immortality of the Soul or Resurrection of the Dead: The Witness of the New Testament," Ingersoll Lecture for

1955, Harvard Divinity School, in Krister Stendahl, ed., *Immortality and Resurrection: Death in the Western World: Two Conflicting Currents of Thought* (New York: Macmillan, 1965).

15. John Bowker writes, "In regarding death as both an enemy and a friend, the religions are, as ever, resisting the fallacy of the falsely dichotomous question." *The Meanings of Death,* p. 209.

16. Tablet X (iii), tr. E. A. Speiser, in James B. Pritchard, ed., *Ancient Near Eastern Texts Relating to the Old Testament,* 3rd ed. (Princeton, NJ: Princeton University Press, 1969).

17. John J. Collins, "Apocalyptic Eschatology as the Transcendence of Death," in Paul D. Hanson, ed., *Visionaries and Their Apocalypses* (Philadelphia: Fortress Press; London: SPCK, 1983), p. 78. On the question of immortality language in early Judaism, see also G. W. E. Nickelsburg, *Resurrection, Immortality, and Eternal Life in Intertestamental Judaism* (Cambridge, MA: Harvard University Press, Harvard Theological Studies 26, 1972).

18. The best guidebook to patristic eschatology is Brian E. Daley, *The Hope of the Early Church* (Cambridge: Cambridge University Press, 1991), a lucid historical survey of the first seven centuries of Christian teachings on death, immortality, resurrection, the *parousia,* and the events of the end times.

19. Psalm 89:48.

20. L. Feer, ed., Samyutta Nikāya 2 (London: Pali Text Society, 1884–98).

21. Sura 21:35.

22. *RB* 4:47. See the annotated Latin and English edition by Timothy Fry, *RB 1980: The Rule of St. Benedict* (Collegeville, MN: Liturgical Press, 1981).

23. Quoted by Winston King, *Zen and the Way of the Sword* (New York: Oxford University Press, 1993), from Daidōji Yūzan Shige-

suki, *The Code of the Samurai,* tr. A. L. Sadler (Rutland, VT: Charles Tuttle, 1988).

24. Some of the material in the next few paragraphs (summarizing the findings of near-death researchers) was presented in a lecture on "Death and Near-Death Today," which I delivered to a conference on "Other Realms: Death, Ecstasy and Otherworldly Journeys in Recent Scholarship" at the University of Chicago Divinity School, May 16, 1991. The text of this lecture appears in John J. Collins and Michael Fishbane, eds., *Death, Ecstasy, and Other Worldly Journeys* (Albany: State University of New York Press, 1995), pp. 379–407.

25. Raymond A. Moody, Jr., *Life After Life: The Investigation of a Phenomenon—Survival of Bodily Death* (New York: Bantam, 1976).

26. See Raymond A. Moody, Jr., *Life After Life, Reflections on Life After Life* (New York: Bantam, 1977), and *The Light Beyond* (New York: Bantam, 1988); Bruce Greyson and Charles Flynn, eds., *The Near-Death Experience* (Springfield, IL: Charles C Thomas, 1984); Kenneth Ring, *Life at Death: A Scientific Investigation of the Near-Death Experience* (New York: Coward, McCann and Geoghegan, 1980), and *Heading Toward Omega: In Search of the Meaning of the Near-Death Experience* (New York: William Morrow, 1984); Michael B. Sabom, *Recollections of Death: A Medical Investigation* (New York: Harper and Row, 1982); George Gallup, Jr., and William Proctor, *Adventures in Immortality: A Look beyond the Threshold of Death* (New York: McGraw-Hill, 1982); Craig Lundahl, ed., *A Collection of Near-Death Research Readings* (Chicago: Nelson-Hall, 1982); Robert Kastenbaum, ed., *Between Life and Death* (New York: Springer, 1979); Melvin Morse, *Closer to the Light* (New York: Villard Books, 1990). Articles on near-death experience have appeared in *The Journal of Nervous and Mental Disease, Lancet, Omega, The American Journal of Psychiatry,* and the *Journal of Near-Death Studies,* edited by Bruce

Greyson and published by Human Sciences Press. *The Journal of Near-Death Studies* is affiliated with the International Association for Near-Death Studies.

27. Discussed in Gallup and Proctor, *Adventures in Immortality.*

28. Moody's master narrative, in *Life After Life,* pp. 21–23: "A man is dying and, as he reaches the point of greatest physical distress, he hears himself pronounced dead by his doctor. He begins to hear an uncomfortable noise, a loud ringing or buzzing, and at the same time feels himself moving very rapidly through a long dark tunnel. After this, he suddenly finds himself outside of his own physical body, but still in the immediate physical environment, and he sees his own body from a distance, as though he is a spectator. He watches the resuscitation attempt from this unusual vantage point and is in a state of emotional upheaval.

"After a while, he collects himself and becomes more accustomed to his odd condition. He notices that he still has a 'body,' but one of a very different nature and with very different powers from the physical body he has left behind. Soon other things begin to happen. Others come to meet and to help him. He glimpses the spirits of relatives and friends who have already died, and a loving, warm spirit of a kind he has never encountered before—a being of light— appears before him. This being asks him a question, nonverbally, to make him evaluate his life and helps him along by showing him a panoramic, instantaneous playback of the major events of his life. At some point he finds himself approaching some sort of barrier or border, apparently representing the limit between earthly life and the next life. Yet, he finds that he must go back to the earth, that the time for his death has not yet come. At this point he resists, for by now he is taken up with his experiences in the afterlife and does not want to return. He is overwhelmed by intense feelings of joy, love, and peace. Despite his attitude, though, he somehow reunites with his physical body and lives.

"Later he tries to tell others, but he has trouble doing so. In the first place, he can find no human words adequate to describe these unearthly episodes. He also finds that others scoff, so he stops telling other people. Still, the experience affects his life profoundly, especially his views about death and its relationship to life."

29. For a discussion of efforts to explain near-death experience, see Carol Zaleski, *Otherworld Journeys: Accounts of Near-Death Experience in Medieval and Modern Times,* rev. ed. (New York: Oxford University Press, 1989), especially chapters 9 and 10.

30. For examples, see I. P. Couliano, *Out of This World: Otherworldly Journeys from Gilgamesh to Albert Einstein* (Boston: Shambhala, 1991); Zaleski, *Otherworld Journeys,* chapter 1; also Lawrence E. Sullivan, *Icanchu's Drum: An Orientation to Meaning in South American Religions* (New York: Macmillan, 1988), pp. 524–48; and the articles in Lawrence E. Sullivan, ed., *Death, Afterlife, and the Soul* (New York: Macmillan, 1989).

Two

1. See the works by Lawrence E. Sullivan previously cited; also Mircea Eliade, *Shamanism: Archaic Techniques of Ecstasy,* tr. Willard Trask (Princeton, NJ: Princeton University Press, 1964).

2. For discussion of the visionary journey motif in Jewish and Christian apocalyptic and mystical literature, see John J. Collins, ed., *Apocalypse: Morphology of a Genre, Semeia* 14 (1979); John J. Collins, *The Apocalyptic Imagination: An Introduction to the Jewish Matrix of Christianity* (New York: Crossroad, 1989); Ioan Petru Culianu, *Psychanodia I: A Survey of the Evidence of the Ascension of the Soul and Its Rel-*

evance (Leiden: Brill, 1983); Mary Dean-Otting, *Heavenly Journeys: A Study of the Motif in Hellenistic Jewish Literature* (Frankfurt, Bern, and New York: Peter Lang, 1984); Ithamar Gruenwald, *Apocalyptic and Merkabah Mysticism* (Leiden: Brill, 1979); David J. Halperin, *The Merkabah in Rabbinic Literature* (New Haven, CT: American Oriental Society, 1980); Martha Himmelfarb, *Tours of Hell: An Apocalyptic Form in Jewish and Christian Literature* (Philadelphia: Fortress Press, 1983); Moshe Idel, *Studies in Ecstatic Kabbalah* (Albany: State University of New York Press, 1988); Susan Niditch, "The Visionary," in G. W. E. Nickelsburg and J. J. Collins, eds., *Ideal Figures in Ancient Judaism* (Missoula, MT: Scholars Press, 1980), pp. 153–79; Christopher Rowland, *The Open Heaven: A Study of Apocalyptic in Judaism and Early Christianity* (New York: Crossroad, 1982); D. S. Russell, *Divine Disclosure: An Introduction to Jewish Apocalyptic* (Minneapolis, MN: Fortress Press, 1992); Alan F. Segal, *Paul the Convert: The Apostolate and Apostasy of Saul the Pharisee* (New Haven, CT, and London: Yale University Press, 1990), especially chapter 2; Alan F. Segal, "Heavenly Ascent in Hellenistic Judaism, Early Christianity, and Their Environments," in *Aufstieg und Niedergang der Römischen Welt, Principat* II, 23, 2 (Berlin: Walter de Gruyter, 1980), pp. 1332–94; James D. Tabor, *Things Unutterable: Paul's Ascent to Paradise in Its Greco-Roman, Judaic, and Early Christian Contexts,* Studies in Judaism (Lanham, MD: University Press of America, 1986).

3. See Jan Bremmer, *The Early Greek Concept of the Soul* (Princeton, NJ: Princeton University Press, 1983).

4. H. G. Evelyn-White, tr., *Hesiod, the Homeric Hymns, and Homerica* (Cambridge, MA: Harvard University Press, 1936), lines 480–82.

5. "The soul [at the point of death] has the same experience as those who are being initiated into the great mysteries." Attributed to Plutarch in Stobaeus, *Anthologion* 4.52.49. Quoted by George E.

Mylonas, *Eleusis and the Eleusinian Mysteries* (Princeton, NJ: Princeton University Press, 1961), p. 264.

6. Quoted by Marvin W. Meyer, ed., *The Ancient Mysteries: A Sourcebook* (New York: Harper and Row, 1987), p. 9.

7. *Stromateis* 3.3.17, quoted by Meyer, ed., *The Ancient Mysteries,* p. 5.

8. Oscar Cullman, "Immortality of the Soul or Resurrection of the Dead," the Ingersoll Lecture for 1955, in Krister Stendahl, ed., *Immortality and Resurrection: Death in the Western World: Two Conflicting Currents of Thought* (New York: Macmillan, 1965), p. 50.

9. Jayne Smith, "Moment of Truth: A Window on Life after Death," videotaped interview, produced by Burke Hully and Mark Remes (Starpath Productions, 1987; distributed by Ozark Video, Springdale, AZ).

10. On the relationship between gender and types of visionary experiences in medieval Europe, see Peter Dinzelbacher, *Vision und Visionsliteratur im Mittelalters* (Stuttgart: Anton Hiersemann, 1981), and *Revelationes* (Turnhout: Brepols, 1991). A wide-ranging scholar of medieval mystical and visionary literature, Dinzelbacher has also examined the parallels and contrasts between medieval and contemporary accounts of near-death experience, in an article on "Mittelalterliche Vision und moderne Sterbeforschung," in *Psychologie in der Mediävistik* (Göppingen, 1985), and in *An der Schwelle zum Jenseits: Sterbevisionen im interkulturellen Vergleich* (Freiburg, 1989).

11. Gregory the Great, *Dialogi,* ed. Umberto Moricca (Rome: Tip. del Senato, 1924). English translation by Odo John Zimmerman (New York: Fathers of the Church, 1959).

12. Bertram Colgrave and R. A. B. Mynors, ed. and tr., *Bede's Ecclesiastical History of the English People* (Oxford: Clarendon Press, 1969).

13. Exod. 33:20.

14. David F. Swenson, tr., *Philosophical Fragments, or A Fragment of Philosophy* (Johannes Climacus) (Princeton, NJ: Princeton University Press, 1936), p. 23.

15. From the hymns *On Faith* (Hymn 31, 2), tr. Sebastian Brock, in the introduction to St. Ephrem's *Hymns on Paradise* (Crestwood, NY: St. Vladimir's Seminary Press, 1990), p. 46.

16. See John Henry Newman, Sermon 2, "The Immortality of the Soul," in *Parochial and Plain Sermons* (San Francisco: Ignatius Press, 1987), p. 15.

17. Jaroslav Pelikan, *The Shape of Death: Life, Death, and Immortality in the Early Fathers* (Nashville, TN, and New York: Abingdon Press, 1961), p. 11.

18. Thanks to Kimberley Patton for reminding me of this text.

19. Bowker, *The Meanings of Death,* p. 221.

20. Miguel de Unamuno, *The Tragic Sense of Life,* tr. J. E. Crawford Flitch (London: Macmillan, 1921; reprint, New York: Dover, 1954), p. 258.

21. John Henry Newman, *An Essay in Aid of a Grammar of Assent,* part II, chap. 8, sect. 2, 6 (Oxford: Oxford University Press, 1985). Commenting on this passage, Newman writes, "Here is an argument for the immortality of the soul. As to its force, be it great or small, will it make a figure in a logical disputation, carried on *secundum artem?* Can any scientific common measure compel the intellects of Dives and Lazarus to take the same estimate of it? [By Dives, Newman means Montaigne, whom he has just been discussing, whose wealth and comfort made him better able to afford skepticism.] Is there any test of the validity of it better than the *ipse dixit* of private judgment, that is, the judgment of those who have a right to judge, and next, the agreement of many private judgments in one and the same view of it?"

22. John Henry Newman, Sermon 10, from *Fifteen Sermons preached before the University of Oxford,* quoted and discussed by Ian Ker, *John Henry Newman: A Biography* (Oxford and New York: Oxford University Press, 1988), p. 260. The theory behind this anecdote is presented in Newman's *An Essay in Aid of a Grammar of Assent.*

In *A Grammar of Consent* (Notre Dame, IN, and London: University of Notre Dame Press, 1991), Aidan Nichols provides the following succinct account of Newman's approach to the question of rational entitlement to religious belief; it is "neither deductive nor, in any strict, formal sense, inferential, as theological rationalists would hold; nor is it couched purely in terms of religious experience straitly so called, as many of their extreme opponents would allege. It is, rather, a cumulation of experiential clues (many of them apparently secular in character) that indicates the reasonableness of assent to the proposition, 'God exists,' although, in the nature of things, these cues cannot compel that assent." P. 1.

23. One thinks immediately of the dialectical theologies of the 1920s (Barth, Bultmann, Brunner, Gogarten); Paul Althaus's landmark book *Die letzten Dinge* (4th ed., 1933; reprint ed., Gütersloh, 1970); Jürgen Moltmann's *Theology of Hope* (New York: Harper and Row, 1967) and *The Crucified God,* tr. R. A. Wilson and John Bowden (New York: Harper and Row, 1974); Gerhard Ebeling's *The Nature of Faith,* tr. Ronald Gregor Smith (Philadelphia: Fortress Press, 1961) and *Word and Faith,* tr. James W. Leitch (Philadelphia: Fortress Press, 1963); Eberhard Jüngel's *Death: The Riddle and the Mystery,* tr. Iain and Ute Nicol (Philadelphia: Westminster Press, 1974) and *God as the Mystery of the World,* tr. Darrell L. Guder (Grand Rapids: Eerdmans, 1983). Emphasis on the revealed character of the doctrine of resurrection (indeed, on the resurrection *as* rev-

elation) is often linked to the rejection of immortality language, but there is no absolute reason why this must be so.

24. A nuanced and learned treatment of this subject can be found in Simon Tugwell, *Human Immortality and the Redemption of Death* (Springfield, IL: Templegate Publishers, 1991), which came into my hands only after I delivered the Meyer Lectures. Tugwell has argued persuasively that "the original message of christianity was not resurrection versus immortality, but hope versus hopelessness" (p. 113), and that the recent practice of pitting resurrection against immortality therefore does an injustice to the complexity of Christian eschatology. A Christian may speak of the soul's continued existence after death without endangering faith in the resurrection, provided he does not propose the *innate* immortality of the soul. I agree wholeheartedly with this position; nonetheless, it is my view that outright rejection of immortality language is too drastic a measure to take, since it risks estranging believers from the literary sources and imaginative resources of their own tradition.

25. See *The Divine Comedy,* vol. 3: *Paradise,* tr. Mark Musa (New York: Penguin Books, 1986), canto 7, line 112, note, p. 91.

26. *Patrologia Graeca* 43: 439–63. English translation from The Office of Readings for Holy Saturday. International Committee on English in the Liturgy, *Liturgy of the Hours,* 1974; reprinted in *The Office of Readings* (Boston: Daughters of St. Paul, 1983), pp. 483–84. My thanks to Paul Burholt for showing me this homily.

27. Sermo Guelferbytanus 3: *Patrologia Latina* 2, 545–46. Thanks to Sister Mariam Malouf, O.S.B., for bringing this to my attention.

28. One of the readings for Morning Prayer on Holy Saturday makes this clear: "None of us lives as his own master and none of us dies as his own master. . . . Both in life and death we are the Lord's.

That is why Christ died and came to life again, that he might be Lord of both the dead and the living" (Rom. 14:7–9).

29. 1 Cor. 15:24, 28; Julian of Norwich, *Showings,* long version, chapter 27: "All shall be well, and all shall be well, and all manner of thing shall be well"; see also chapters 29, 32–34, 86.

30. Colleen McDannell and Bernhard Lang, *Heaven: A History* (New Haven, CT, and London: Yale University Press, 1988).

31. Robert Jay Lifton, "On Death and Continuity," in *The Life of the Self* (New York: Simon and Schuster, 1976), pp. 32–33. One of my students, upon reading Lifton's list of the five kinds of symbolic immortality, remarked, "but he left out shopping!"

32. D. Z. Phillips, *Death and Immortality* (London and Basingstoke: Macmillan, 1970), pp. 66–78.

Three

1. "Letter on Certain Questions Concerning Eschatology," Sacred Congregation for the Doctrine of the Faith, *L'Osservatore Romano* (July 23, 1979), pp. 7–8.

2. Affirming "continuation and subsistence" may not be the same thing as affirming "immortality of the soul." Simon Tugwell suggests that the letter reflects some hesitation about immortality language (*Human Immortality,* p. 176). The wording of the letter appears to me to leave the question open, however, rather than to warrant the rejection of immortality language.

3. There are some exceptions among contemporary philosophers and theologians; for example, philosopher Richard Swinburne has developed a sustained defense of anthropological dualism in *The Evolution of the Soul* (Oxford: Clarendon Press, 1986) and elsewhere. For present purposes, however, the current philosophical debates for and

against dualism can be set aside. My defense of soul talk and of dualistic imagery rests on other grounds. I am concerned with the imagistic character and power of religious language, and consider it possible for dramatically dualistic religious language to coexist with a variety of holistic philosophical anthropologies.

4. Victimae paschali laudes immolent Christiani.

Agnus redemit oves:

Christus innocens Patri reconciliavit peccatores.

Mors et vita duello conflixere mirando:

dux vitae mortuus, regnat vivus.

5. "The Tenth Hymn: A Hymn for the Burial of the Dead," lines 1–32, in Harold Isbell, ed., *The Last Poets of Imperial Rome* (Harmondsworth: Penguin, 1971), pp. 198–99.

6. See Phillips, *Death and Immortality,* pp. 43–47.

7. Antony Flew, "Death," in Antony Flew and Alasdair Macintyre, eds., *New Essays in Philosophical Theology* (London: SCM Press, 1950), p. 270.

8. Joseph Ratzinger, *Eschatologie—Tod und ewiges Leben* (Regensburg: Friedrich Pustet Verlag, 1977). Available in English, with added preface and afterword, as *Eschatology: Death and Eternal Life,* tr. Michael Waldstein; translation edited by Aidan Nichols (Washington, DC: Catholic University Press, 1988), pp. 107–9.

9. See, for example, Karl Barth, *The Resurrection of the Dead,* tr. H. J. Stenning (New York: Fleming H. Revell, 1933); Karl Rahner, "The Hermeneutics of Eschatological Assertions," in *Theological Investigations* IV, tr. Kevin Smyth (London: Darton, Longman and Todd, 1966; reprint ed., New York: Crossroad, 1982), pp. 323–46; and "The Life of the Dead," in *Theological Investigations,* pp. 345–54; Karl Rahner, *On the Theology of Death* (New York: Seabury, 1973); Helmut Thielicke, *Death and Life,* tr. Edward H. Schroeder

(Philadelphia: Fortress Press, 1970); Eberhard Jüngel, *Death: The Riddle and the Mystery*, tr. Iain and Ute Nicol (Philadelphia: Westminster Press, 1974); Gisbert Greshake, *Auferstehung der Toten* (Essen, 1969). Among the many issues raised by the controversy over immortality and resurrection, the resurrection-in-death model has been the subject of especially vigorous debate during the past decade. See Gisbert Greshake and G. Lohfink, *Naherwartung-Auferstehung-Unsterblichkeit* (Freiburg, 1986); Gisbert Greshake and Jacob Kremer, *Resurrectio mortuorum* (Darmstadt: Wissenschaftliche Buchgesellschaft, 1986), pp. 168–276; and Ratzinger, *Eschatology*, pp. 108–12 and appendix II, "Afterword to the English Edition," pp. 261–74. Cardinal Ratzinger quotes with alarm the following passage from the *Dutch Catechism:* "Existence after death is already something like the resurrection of the new body" (p. 108).

10. See Zaleski, *Otherworld Journeys*, pp. 116–17.

11. See Peter Metcalf and Richard Huntington, *Celebrations of Death: The Anthropology of Mortuary Ritual*, 2nd ed. (Cambridge: Cambridge University Press, 1991), which provides a survey of contemporary ethnographic studies on practices of secondary burial and other death rituals, as well as a reappraisal of the theoretical work of Robert Hertz and Arnold van Gennep.

12. Discussed in Metcalf and Huntington, *Celebrations of Death.* For a fascinating modern example of mourning rites involving reburial, see Loring M. Danforth, *The Death Rituals of Rural Greece* (Princeton, NJ: Princeton University Press, 1982).

13. Plutarch, *Moralia* 166C, "Of Superstition."

14. Hans Urs von Balthasar, *Was dürfen wir hoffen?* (Einsiedeln: Johannes Verlag, 1986), and *Kleiner Diskurs über Hölle* (Ostfildern: Schwabenverlag, 1987); available together in English in *Dare We Hope "That All Men Be Saved"? with a Short Discourse on Hell*, tr.

David Kipp and Lothar Krauth (San Francisco: Ignatius Press, 1988). See also his *Theodramatik* IV (Einsiedeln: Johannes Verlag, 1983) (English translation forthcoming from Ignatius Press).

15. For illuminating treatment of patristic teachings on the hope for universal restoration, see Gerhart B. Ladner, *The Idea of Reform: Its Impact on Christian Thought and Action in the Age of the Fathers* (Cambridge, MA: Harvard University Press, 1959); and Brian E. Daley, *The Hope of the Early Church,* especially chapter 11, pp. 168–204.

16. Some of the material in the following three paragraphs (citing examples of the life review) was presented previously in a lecture on "Death and Near-Death Today," delivered to a conference on "Other Realms: Death, Ecstasy and Otherworldly Journeys in Recent Scholarship" at the University of Chicago Divinity School, May 16, 1991. The text of this lecture appears in John J. Collins and Michael Fishbane, eds., *Death, Ecstasy, and Other Worldly Journeys* (Albany: State University of New York Press, 1995), pp. 383–407.

17. Thomas De Quincey, *Confessions of an English Opium-Eater,* quoted by Russell Noyes, Jr., "Dying and Mystical Consciousness," *Journal of Thanatology* (January–February 1971), p. 30.

18. Quoted by Noyes in "Dying and Mystical Consciousness," p. 29.

19. Albert Heim, "Notizen über den Tod durch Absturz," *Jahrbuch des schweizer alpen Club* 27 (1892), pp. 327–37. Translated by Russell Noyes, Jr., and Roy Kletti in "The Experience of Dying from Falls," *Omega* 2 (1972), pp. 45–52.

20. Robert N. Butler, "The Life Review: An Integration of Reminiscence in the Aged," *Psychiatry* 26 (1963): 65–76. See also Robert N. Butler and M. I. Lewis, *Aging and Mental Health: Positive Psychological Approaches* (St. Louis, MO: C. V. Mosby, 1973).

21. Colin M. Parkes, *Bereavement: Studies of Grief in Adult Life* (New York: International Universities Press, 1972).

22. On death as decisive for personal identity, see Ladislaus Boros, *Mysterium Mortis: Der Mensch in seiner letzten Entscheidung* (Olten, 1967). In English: *The Mystery of Death* (New York: Seabury, 1965). See also Boros, "Death: A Theological Reflection," in Michael J. Taylor, ed., *The Mystery of Suffering and Death* (New York: Doubleday, 1974), "The New Heaven and the New Earth," and "Regarding the Theology of Death," in Wolfdieter Theurer, ed., *Readings in Christian Eschatology* (Derby, NY: Society of St. Paul, 1966).

23. P. M. H. Atwater, *I Died Three Times in 1977* (Dayton, VA, 1980), p. 22. See also her fuller account in *Coming Back to Life* (New York: Ballantine Books, 1988).

24. English translation from the "The Office of Compline," Stanbrook Abbey, Worcester, England.

25. Note that this simple act of entrusting oneself to God could not be accomplished with such economy and grace if it had to make do without the imaginative dualism of body and soul.

26. English translation from "The Office of Compline."

27. *De civitate Dei,* book 22, chapter 30.